A Book of Gentleness

A Book of Gentleness

Gary Spanovich

J O H N   H O N E A   P U B L I S H I N G

Illustrations by Jason Zeringue

Copyright © 1995 by Gary Spanovich
Library of Congress Cataloging
in Publication Data:
Spanovich, Gary
A Book of Gentleness

94-079791
ISBN   0-9636072-5-1

"I found Gary Spanovich's book: A Book of Gentleness, to be very inspirational. Such a book helps in these times when there seems to be much hopelessness and helplessness. As Gary says, we must let God take over and we must let go.

I found the meditation process to be helpful in both giving me inner peace and making my heart more compassionate toward others.

Gary's book should bring you greater peace in Christ and greater concern for others."

Henri LaCerte,
O.S.B., Ph.D., S.T.D., J.C.D., D. Min.

"Along with the Scriptures, sometimes a literary work beacons our 'Inner Light' to shine forth to enlighten ourselves and those around us. The work by Gary Spanovich entitled A Book of Gentleness, can help an individual aspire to recognizing the 'Light of Christ' within one's self."

Timothy Barker,

Dedication

*I dedicate this book to the Holy Spirit
of Jesus Christ who is the Truth and the
Light and who is within all: To the
Creator. my true Father without whom I
would be nothing for He is all; and to the
Earth. my true Mother. for without her my
healing would not have taken place. You
have my eternal love and gratitude.*

Table of Contents

Table of Illustrations

Table of Meditations

Foreward

Sitting here in Tucson, Arizona watching the snow come down outside my window I'm struck with the unlikeliness of this vacation. My vacation started out as two weeks in the sun in Death Valley, California for a little outdoor purification and rest from my life in the Pacific Northwest.

As always with trips for those purposes I seek out the desert; a place of great natural beauty, emptiness, and quietness. It is in that place of quietness that I feel I connect into the "I" of myself most deeply. It is always into the desert that I go in order to feel the presence of the Creator. In the desert one can even hear a slight hum from the Earth as it vibrates to the one cosmic tune.

The desert, as well as the wilderness and the natural areas of the earth, are where I feel closest to God and they are where I go regularly to renew myself and to commune directly with the still small voice within. It is in the earth's natural areas that I feel I connect into our Creator most deeply. It is in these natural earth areas that all can feel the *Presence of God.*

Following a deep meditation, within myself the words were spoken, "Go south, go where it is warm, go to Tucson." The next morning I packed my car and sat in the nearby hot springs one more time with some other desert dwellers. As the wind began to pick up and blow the sand, I thought I was just being guided to a place of being more comfortable. My friend Tom, who was with me, felt I was being guided to Tucson to meet a teacher. One thing was sure, as we left the desert and listened to the radio, we were just in front of a massive winter storm front.

I dropped Tom off in Beatty to catch a bus back to Reno and headed for Tucson. As I drove I felt in my being a very intense attraction there. I didn't know what would happen, just that I was to be in Tucson for the remainder of my vacation. My inner voice also told me to begin fasting for three days.

As I approached the city, my inner guidance directed me to a hotel, which felt good to me. On checking in I did another deep meditation and it became clear that I was to begin writing this book. The beginning of the book was my sole purpose for being in Tucson.

As I meditated, my inner voice spoke the twelve chapter titles of this book to me:

1. **In The Beginning:** *To speak about the separation of humankind from God.*

2. **For God So Loved, God Created Love:** *For God's greatest gift to humankind is the gift of love.*

3. **The Earthly Delight:** *Each of us are stewards of one of God's greatest creations, the earth.*

4. **World Without End:** *Each of us individually is on a life journey toward wholeness and integration.*

5. **The Disciples:** *We all share a deep spiritual brotherhood and sisterhood in this human family we find ourselves in.*

6. **The Coming Of The Lord:** *The Creator is speaking to all of us constantly from within and He can be heard as a still small voice.*

7. **The Dawn Of Tomorrow:** *God has a glorious vision for humankind and the earth.*

8. **The Christ Within:** *God's sacred voice speaking from deep within each of us will lead us to Christ consciousness.*

9. **The Christ Without:** *The light of the Christ consciousness dwells within all souls and we must seek that light in all our brothers and sisters.*

10. **And God Created All People Equal:** *We are all loved equally by God and we must open to seeing God in all creation.*

11. **The Future Is Now:** *It is time to acknowledge our individual journey toward God, whatever its form, and start our spiritual work.*

12. **God Is Calling All People To His Ministry:** *All souls are God's ministers and each of us has a calling and a role to play.*

I felt guided to spend the next three days in my hotel room to begin writing this book, a somewhat unlikely way to spend a vacation.

Namaste
Tucson, Arizona

Introduction

I offer my love to you. I write this book from my heart and soul and from the love of God which fills me. I offer it to you with a prayer that through reading it and practicing the meditations you, too, will be filled with a love of God. It is out of God's love and the in–dwelling Christ Spirit within all that these words and meditations have come to me to offer out to others.

I can testify to you that if you will love God with all your being, God will transform your life and bring you a life that is filled with more growth, joy, and love. Keep your attention on your love of God and know that God is in all.

The message of this book is that you don't have to nor should you do your life alone through this *great transition* time we are in, for God is within you and within every person. God wishes you to turn to God now, and to per-sonally assist you, two great gifts have already been given to you and they are both within yourself. One is the still small voice of God and the other is the holy light, the Christ Light which is deep within you. Love is the key you must use to unlock both these gifts fully.

The still small voice of God is like a road map within yourself that whispers to you about how to get through a dark inner forest. By opening your heart to God and listen-ing to the still small voice within, you will know where to turn on your personal life journey so as not to get lost and confused. The holy light within you is like a powerful flash-light which God has personally given you to see in the dark so you won't stumble and get panicky through these times. These gifts are already within you and they are available to all no matter what religion you follow or what culture you come from.

Our personal work is to open our hearts by following Christ's age old advice to us: "Love God above all," and "Love your neighbor as yourself." By following your own personal path of the heart, which is our own personal path of love, you will open yourself fully to God.

By personally spending quiet time within and feeling the *Presence of God* within yourself, you will begin to hear the still small voice and to experience the holy light and you will be able to find peace in your life. For you will find it within yourself, not outside yourself,so it will have a lasting effect; and you will find it thanks to the Grace of God, with God's help, not depending solely upon yourself. From that place of peace you will be able to go out into the world and offer peace and love to others in God's name. You will allow yourself to *go to work* for God, and God's work will bring you the deepest fulfillment you can experience in this lifetime. If there is a Universal teaching for the times we are now living in, perhaps that teaching is "we can't do it without God." Now is the time to turn to God for help with your personal life journey.

The *Presence of God* is a mystical experience. When we feel within ourselves the *Divine presence* we are transported from this everyday reality to another reality, the *Spiritual reality*. It is not that we physically leave, rather within us we are able to dwell in the *Divine presence* and at the same time still remain in this world, going about our everyday work. Through this simultaneous embracing of our *everyday reality* and the experiencing within our being of the *Divine presence of God*, we truly become God's instruments on earth, for we are able to open to all God is. By each of us *dwelling in God* we allow God to flow out from each of us, doing the Divine will through us.

This book is intended to help you feel God within your–

self, so that you can then know God intimately. The book also explains why it is important to take the time now and *go inside yourself* and to listen to the still small voice of God, as well as experience the seed of Christ Light that is within you. Rather than concentrating on the separations which exist in individual lives, this book, through its words, sketches and meditations, offers you a way to explore your own sacred connection directly with God no matter who you are or where you come from or what religion you follow.

The book contains a self-guided meditation following the end of each of the twelve chapters. The meditations will take you deeper within yourself. Meditation is the basic tool you can use to hear the sacred voice of God within yourself. It has often been said that *meditation* is the process we use to listen to God and *prayer* is the process we use to talk to God. It's as if we knock on God's door with our prayers, and meditation is when God answers us.

You could also have someone read the meditations to you while you close your eyes and go deep inside, listening to the still small voice, and then in turn read the meditations for the other person while they listen inside.

You might also do a meditation with a group, having someone read the meditation to the entire group. I encourage you to try both, doing them alone as well as with people you feel close to and who also desire to connect with God in this personal and intimate way.

I encourage you to keep a personal journal. The experiences that come to you directly from God are very personal and intimate. At difficult times in your life it will be a source of inspiration and stability to read the words the Lord has spoken directly to you from deep within your being.

In this book you will read "He," "She," "Her," "Him" in relation to God. I felt no male or female gender in association with the word Him or Her as the book came to me. Other words are also used such as the Lord, Christ, Mystery, the Oneness. I encourage you as you read this book to substitute your own word for God, simply recognizing that whatever word you use, God is the Creator of all.

These are momentous times we are presently living in and it is God that we must individually and collectively turn to if we are to know how to steer through these times. God is here to guide us, all of us, and can be heard by all as a still small voice and experienced as a holy light within. It is the still small voice that we must begin to listen to, and it is our inner Christ Light we must focus on if we are to know what direction to take in our lives, and it is love that will open us fully to God.

Chapter One

In The Beginning

"Come To Me First. Always"

*I*n the beginning was God and out of God all creation was created. It is only because of God's light and God's love that all humanity exists today. It is only through God's light and God's love that humanity can be brought to wholeness and returned home to God. The *Light of God* is coming and it will enliven all of us and lift us up to God. It is God to whom we must always remember to pay homage. It is through the gentle still small voice of God which speaks from deep within the silence of our being that we can each know of the coming of the *Light of God* and how to prepare for it, personally and collectively.

In the beginning was God, Oneness, I , Him, Her, One, Light. In the beginning was, and always will be, God. The material Universe was created out of formless oneness in a massive explosion of love and light. Out of the One consciousness came all consciousness. All form that was created out of the One consciousness retained the One consciousness in the beginning.

At some point, parts of the One consciousness which had created itself as form, began to feel itself to be separate and distinct. In place of the One consciousness, awareness of self, awareness of a separate existence began to grow and to perpetuate itself.

The One consciousness still existed and always will exist, but now what resided in form was an awareness of self or self-consciousness; that is, a self-consciousness of separateness of forms separate from other forms. As this awareness of self, separate from the One consciousness grew, it began to reoccur.

Out of this separateness of existence came the desire to create more separateness, and yet in the beginning there was both consciousness of the Oneness along with awareness of self. Gradually through life after life, self-awareness became dominant and consciousness of Oneness receded to a very small place within a mortal being. And yet the Oneness never left, as it is the Oneness that provides the life force for all existence. It is the God consciousness that spins the planets, that continues the outward expansion of the Universe, that allows our lungs to breathe or our kidneys to function without our thinking about it.

In place of God consciousness, man and woman have filled themselves with self-awareness or human consciousness. In filling themselves with self-awareness, like a full vase, each has left little room for God consciousness. Man and woman's self-awareness is so full, there is not much room left for the Oneness. And yet the life force still functions in man and woman, the God consciousness is still there; it just exists where man and woman have not taken their self-awareness, such as in the breathing of their lungs and the beating of their heart. Every moment this God consciousness creates miracles in every human body. If the God consciousness did not make our hearts beat, what would?

As we humans focus more and more on our separateness from the Oneness, we deepen the illusion of ourselves separate from one another. In our focus on the separateness of our forms and all other forms, we reinforce form and self and weaken God consciousness. And yet again, God consciousness is always there; just ask yourself, "What makes my heart beat?"

Today, humankind, that is the collection of all humans that are alive today, stands at a crossroad. One path will lead to the ultimate destruction of humankind. This path is the path of fear and further separateness from the Oneness, from God consciousness. On this journey man and woman will give new definition to separateness. In their separateness they will destroy human life as it is known today. Separateness cannot create, only destroy. Only the Oneness can create.

Today, humankind has the opportunity to move toward love, toward God consciousness. On this path, which is the path of love and light, humankind will experience God consciousness on a grand scale. On this path, the awareness of separateness of form will gradually fall away and be replaced with awareness of Oneness of God.

As a separate world unto himself, each person stands individually at a crossroad. For each of us the choice is real and made manifest in our lives through our thoughts, words, behavior, feelings; so go each of us, in choosing a path of fear or a path of love, so goes the human race collectively. Humankind, individually as well as collectively, stands on the brink of a new tomorrow. A tomorrow that is pregnant with either unimaginable glory and love or one populated with unimaginable terror and pain.

The human race will not decide which path to take, because the human race is you. Only you in your self–awareness and separateness can choose for yourself. And as you choose for yourself, so the human race chooses.

No one can intercede for any of us, not our friends, relatives, government, nor will the God consciousness to which we deeply long to return to. In our separateness we must decide our own path through this life. Either to return to our state of love or choose further fear and let the natural rhythm of fear take us to its inevitable final conclusion.

One thousand years ago, when there were fewer people on the planet, the collective power of our fear was less than it is today. Wars, destruction, the taking of life occurred, and yet on a far lesser scale than the last 50 years. Today, with humankind populating every nook and cranny of our planet, the power of our fear is awesome. The power of our fear, if given full vent, will destroy the human species. On the other hand, the power of billions of separate individuals deciding to return to love, to light, and to God consciousness will truly be a miraculous sight.

The human species having nuclear weapons, in its present state of God consciousness, is like a five–year–old child playing with lighted matches in a room full of open gasoline cans. The child simply does not have the consciousness to behave appropriately. An adult in this same situation would have the wherewithal to behave differently, safely, posing no threat to themselves or to anyone else.

The human species has evolved and is evolving, and God evolves humanity through us individually. Only we, in our separateness of forms and in our self–awareness, can undertake the journey home to Oneness, to God consciousness. As we individually choose that path of love and light, so will humankind. There is a critical mass of individual choice towards God consciousness that is needed. Once this critical mass is reached, one way or another, the momentum and the direction of humanity will be decided.

Often times prophecies speak of the second coming of the Christ and the coming of the anti-Christ. The anti-Christ is fear given power by humanity, by individual choice to move away from God consciousness into separateness. The second coming of the Christ is God consciousness given power by humanity, by individual choice to move toward the love and the light of God in our personal lives.

By individually choosing to see through the falseness and illusion of our fear into the Oneness of love, we will experience a rapture, a blessed feeling of something like ecstasy. In this deep spiritual experience all boundaries and blockages will begin to drop away. In this deep place of Spirit it will be impossible to feel anger or hurt or pain, only the rapture of feeling God consciousness within us. It is the same rapture that Christ felt.

To start this process, to decide in favor of God consciousness, it will take a leap on our part. A leap of faith, to go from the purely material to the purely spiritual and then back again, transmuting the material reality into the spiritual reality.

The material world we have created and which God has created for us is a powerful attention-getter. In order to connect to the Holy Spirit we must go beyond the material, we must transcend the material. This is not easy to do, especially when we have never done it or even thought about doing it. By what mystery does the bridging of the material and spiritual gap occur? Through the mystery of going deep within ourself and knocking on the door of our Godself where we can see the holy light of God within and listen to the still small voice of God speaking, and by opening our hearts to the "Spirit of Christ" that is indwelling there.

In spite of the material world and the appearance of separateness, all of us, as human souls, are on our upward expansion toward full God consciousness. All of us are in our own individual process, and only God consciousness, within our being, knows where we are on our journey. No one can judge us from the outside, only God, for only God truly knows us and knows our struggle.

On this journey we are constantly confronted with all manner of material roadblocks. Material occurrences which hold our attention to the point of suffocation of the Holy Spirit within us. And yet the Holy Spirit cannot be suffocated, it is not of the material world, it is beyond.

We are not our form, we are our consciousness. Our God consciousness created our form and our human consciousness has taken credit. Like a five–year–old child who has just created his or her first water color painting, we are justifiably proud. If our God consciousness can create our form, consider what miracles we could create by residing fully in our God consciousness.

And really there is no *our own consciousness*, there is only consciousness, and that is the One consciousness. What there is, is the *illusion of separateness and fear* which we individually and collectively have given power to. By choosing God we take power away from the illusion and give the power to God.

Focusing on our form places our attention and our power in a finite place. The form, the physicality, will pass away; that we know, not the consciousness. The consciousness is not of this world, it simply creates in this world. Our world is like a blank canvas where God consciousness has come and painted a very beautiful picture. One day our canvas will be wiped clean and God consciousness will paint another scene.

The creation of the human consciousness by the God consciousness is but one small step on humankind's long journey from Oneness to Oneness. The rhythm of the dance of God is constantly playing through humankind's evolutionary journey. Those who stop to hear the music of God and feel God's rhythm live very different lives than those who do not. Their lives are ones of love, of magic, of aliveness, of joy, of freshness, for their dance is not bound by the limitations of humankind. Man and woman are bound by themselves; God is not bound–God is limitless.

Those who choose not to hear the music of God also dance to their own tune in life. Their dance is one of right and wrong, of judgment, of always being slightly unsure and off center and of always sensing intuitively a missing piece in their lives. It is in the sensing of this missing piece that so much misdirected and misguided energy is expended.

Like a mother hen searching frantically for one of her brood that has disappeared, one searches with all one's intensity and ignorance because one is not even aware for what one searches. Because the material world presents an obvious place to look, one searches most easily there. Also, man and woman look around and see others searching frantically in the material world, and this lends credence to their own search, this reinforces their journey.

Human consciousness is a little like our friends the lemmings. As one lemming throws itself off a cliff in its ignorance, mimicking the ignorance of another lemming, so humans follow the ignorance of other humans, rarely questioning the collective human consciousness. The collective human consciousness has a lemming–like quality to it.

Others do not search in the strictly material world, rather they search deeper, in the darkness of humankind's separation from God. To search in the separation brings the harshest lessons in life and the most pain and agony for the human soul. This is less a dance than a seizure of the human spirit.

And yet all human creation goes through a beginning and ending process. There are no exceptions to this, for this is one of God's greatest teachings. For humankind to put their focus on only human consciousness is to see existence as beginning at birth and ending at death. This deepens the illusion of the separation from God. If man's existence ends at death, there is no safety here. How can man or woman relax into the safety of life if he or she believes it will be taken from them? How can an innocent trusting five-year-old child, who depends on all her sustenance coming from her parents, feel safe if she knows that one day her warm cozy home and loving parents will be no more and she will be thrust to make her way alone on some inner-city street? Can she ever again, with that thought, relax into the arms of her warm loving parents without feeling the pain of her eventual separation?

Such is the state of humankind, the human consciousness, which believes that its limited experience of life is all there is, and that one day that will be taken from it. This is not the case of God consciousness, for God has no beginning nor end, God simply Is. God is with us now and it is God we journey to when we pass from this life.

By placing their focus and attention in human consciousness, man and woman are defining their experience of life in the most limited and narrow of ways. It is in this limited definition that the harsh lessons are taught and learned, for there is no true safety within these narrow limits.

By placing their focus and attention in God consciousness, man and woman define their experience in the truth, in the abundance, joy and love of life. They open their individual lives to Is-ness and Unlimitedness, they open their human consciousness to the Christ consciousness that dwells within them, ever willing to show them their individual path to full God realization. That is why the indwelling Christ Spirit is the wayshower: He alone shows the way.

God Is: God is in the moment. In each moment, humans define their experience of life by where they place their attention. The most saintly of persons may place his or her attention on God for forty years, and then for whatever reason, they put their focus on human consciousness, and sometimes very hard lessons are both taught and learned in that one moment. And yet God knows all hearts and God compensates the loving heart, no matter what words are spoken or acts undertaken, for love always protects. There is no coasting, there is no momentum built up for those forty years that will prevent a lesson from taking place when one has turned their back on God consciousness, if even for a moment. For that choice is of the human consciousness and so is its experience.

It is unwholeness which causes a human soul to shift its focus from God consciousness. It is a human being's lack of healing which creates many of life's harshest lessons. All who are on this earth plane have come to heal unhealed parts of their physical, emotional, spiritual bodies. In that healing, all blocks to the full opening to God consciousness may be dissolved.

It is a person's unhealed emotional, physical, or spiritual aspect which blocks him or her from seeing the truth of an action taken from a place of separation. It is the ego's hold that prevents them from confessing their action or even realizing it themselves. The ego is an aspect of the creation of the separation, the separation from God.

We may experience our unhealed aspects in either a conscious God choosing way or an unconscious separation choosing manner. To experience our unhealed aspects in an unconscious manner is to often project our unwholeness outside of ourselves, on to someone, some thing, or some situation. This happens because the human consciousness is unable to own the unhealed aspect directly and too ignorant to realize what they are doing in seeing the aspect reflected in another. The reflection may or may not be there. If two people are seeing the same reflection and projecting their unwholeness upon another, then they are both attempting to heal themselves in ignorance. Often the taking of life, war or great pain is caused when two or more people unite in separation and unconsciousness.

Likewise, the projection of an unhealed aspect might be onto a perfect mirror. Jesus Christ was such a perfect mirror. The Christ consciousness that Jesus realized became a perfect mirror for all the unhealed aspects of those who lived in His time. Many priests and ministers looked upon Christ, the perfect mirror, during His day and saw hatred, blasphemy, and other unhealed parts of themselves. In their ignorance they were not capable of realizing these were all aspects of themselves that Christ, in His perfection, was reflecting to them. So it was also later in history with the church inspired Inquisition, or anytime in history where man or woman has looked at another, and seeing either their reflection or their judgment of what they are seeing, has sought to condemn or harm another. They have believed that what they see is not an aspect of who they are, but rather is fully outside of themselves; this is never true.

To experience our unhealed aspects in a conscious manner is to have a very different experience. When we choose God consciousness we choose to truly heal those aspects of ourselves. For God guides us to higher and higher places of love and understanding, as the blocks within ourselves slowly dissolve at the Creator's gentle urging. To choose consciousness as we seek to heal ourselves is to know all in our lives is a reflection of our selves. It is to own what we see, to love what we see, to forgive what we see, and to ask the Creator to guide us to a new level of love and life.

It is an individual's lack of healing which blocks him or her from seeing the truth. It is the choice of God consciousness which propels an individual soul toward his or her own healing guided by the Spirit of Christ and it is through the heart that this indwelling Spirit of Christ can be realized.

The next two decades on the planet will be difficult decades for the human experience. They will be glorious decades for the God experience. There will be much suffering within the human experience and the human consciousness. Things always assumed and depended upon, in human terms, will shift and change, creating great fear and hysteria. Men and women who choose to have a purely human experience of life will be shaken.

Men and women who have chosen to open their hearts to a God experience of life, within themselves, will find their human experience flowing and joyful. God will guide these souls through the darkness of these next two decades. It is as if these individuals will appear to be walking on water, when in reality, tall, stable poles will go down to the ocean floor and rise up to slightly below the water surface. To others looking, it appears people are walking on water, it appears as a miracle. To those who are listening to God's voice within themselves, it will not be a miracle, for they trust God to guide their footstep to the next pillar. They themselves do not see the pillar under the water, they just trust God with all their heart and know God will guide their next footstep. They are listening to the still small voice of God within.

And yet God's still small voice is in the moment, and so there will be times when even those who choose God will either not follow God's voice or turn their attention somewhere else. Sometimes a footstep will be placed on water where there is no pillar, and a person will fall into the sea. No matter, that person will know that they simply did not pay attention to the still small voice of God within them. They will know those great rock pillars are there, and they will simply reach out and place their arms around them, for they will know they are only one footstep away. Once they have grabbed one, their balance and sense of well being will return, for again they will experience God's guidance within themselves. And so they will simply climb back up onto the pillars and continue walking through life, allowing God's voice to direct their every step toward light and wholeness.

This will be a very different experience than those who have not chosen to hear God's voice within themselves. For them the world will at times be a truly frightening place. It will be like being thrown overboard from a ship at sea in a tremendous storm, with thunder, lightning, great waves, and wind throwing their individual life around. They will be scared and bewildered by this experience. They will not focus on God, so their only experience will be that of which their human experience tells them. Past human experience will not be of much help, none will have been through this storm. Now and then boats will come by, and captains of these ships will say, "Follow me, come aboard," and people will climb aboard, grateful for even the slightest comfort. Some of these captains will be honest and say they speak for themselves, others will be dishonest and say they speak for the Lord.

There will be no true safety in grabbing the hand of these captains: this will be a place of false rescue, for their boats will eventually be sunk in the storm. These captains have the same lesson as those adrift in the sea, to choose God fully and to obey God. No one need speak for God to others, when all can hear God within themselves.

So, within this raging storm there will be many different life experiences: those who open their hearts to love and follow God's voice within themselves and appear to be walking on water; those who are adrift and fully within their human experience; those who will wish to speak for the Lord to other people, telling them what to do and where to go and how to live; and finally all combinations of the above experiences. The earth plane will truly be a confusing place to be for awhile.

And yet there is no confusion in God, for God Is. God is love, God is joy, God is freedom, God is the pulsing of lifeforce through all form, for all form is God's creation. To experience God consciousness within one's own being is to experience the most profound ecstasy imaginable. An ecstasy that is every human soul's birthright.

The first step, on the journey toward this explosion of God within oneself, is to choose God, first, always. God can be chosen in whatever way is appropriate to an individual. It could be: "God, please come into my life"; or "God, I love you"; or "God, help me"; or "God, where are you?" It matters not the words used. Just the clear yearning and opening of the human heart in love for connection to the Creator. One can use the word God, or Jehovah, or Krishna, or Christ within our being. God knows the intent, knows the love in the heart that speaks, irrelevant to the words used. Words are for man; God Is.

Once a soul has chosen to seek God in this lifetime, the next step is to open to hearing God's still small voice within oneself. Then guidance may come as a voice, as images, as knowingness, as imagination, as feeling, as a physical sensation. God will communicate to us in different ways for we are different individuals. Hearing and feeling God's guidance within ourselves is one of the clearest, direct transmissions of Divine Grace that any human soul may expect to experience in a lifetime. It is part of the Christ experience, for God spoke directly to Jesus Christ.

Hearing God's guidance for us through another person is fraught with difficulties and is the rich, fertile ground of many of our most intense spiritual tests and lessons. It is also inappropriate for the present age which is upon us, an age when all can experience Divine revelation and God consciousness by opening to the sacred voice within.

In opening to God's still small voice within ourselves we must be as children: innocent, open, vulnerable. If we experience resistance then we need to do healing, for resistance is a call to healing within ourselves. Our resistance will hamper and create static in our direct communication with the Creator. If we can but open to God's presence within us and be like little children, then God will guide us in our life journey through all our blocks. We must simply trust God's still small voice within ourselves and have faith in God.

Sometimes our unhealed and unwhole parts will speak, and we will follow, believing it is God's voice, and perhaps we will fall back into the sea off the pillar. No matter, we will reach out again, climb back on the pillar and God will guide us to our wholeness and to God. God Is in the moment, so every moment God must be chosen for God's guidance to have power in our life. In the beginning was Oneness, I, Him, Her. In the beginning, was and always will be, God, the Lord, the Creator of all.

In order to choose God we must seek to dwell in the *presence of God* and the wholeness that choice brings. It is through dwelling in *God's presence* that we can feel whole within ourselves and at peace inside. The following meditation will assist you in choosing the *wholeness of God* within.

"Come To Me First. Always"

MEDITATION ON CHOOSING WHOLENESS IN GOD

INTENT

This meditation will assist you in choosing *wholeness in God.* For we are whole beings when we choose to dwell in the presence of God. We can sometimes forget to *feel the presence of God* and, as a result, our *inner emotional connections* can become cloudy and need a clearing out. This meditation will assist you to feel your inner wholeness in the *presence of God.*

SUGGESTED ENVIRONMENT

Create an environment that is very warm and nurturing for yourself and which will bring you the greatest peace and comfort. This is very important for it will give you the safety you will need to go within your being and to feel at a deep emotional level. It could be done inside in a quiet darkened room, with a candle burning to symbolize the *Light of God*. If doing the meditation alone, ensure it is a place where you will not be interrupted or distracted. Keep a journal handy in which to write down your experiences, visions and feelings so you can review them regularly.

HOW TO BEGIN

Begin with the following steps:

❧ First, find a comfortable position where your spine can be straight, either in a comfortable chair or lying on the floor.

❧ Second, close your eyes and do some simple deep breathing for a few minutes, releasing everything that has occurred previously in the day. The deep breathing is very important.

❧ Third, adopt an open, meditative attitude by simply reaffirming to yourself that you are open and listening to God.

❧ Fourth, focus your attention on the moment and quiet any lingering thoughts. Just become aware of your breathing and your body. Begin to repeat the following affirmation (or one of your own) to yourself silently: "I Am Open To Feeling My Wholeness." If you are a visual person, try focusing on an image of a shining white light.

THE MEDITATION

With your eyes still closed become aware of your body and its weight pressing down. Next, focus on your personality and all its different aspects: your shyness, your clarity, your sense of humor, etc. Just reflect on who you are as a person. Next, reflect on your emotional self and the complete range of your emotions, both dark and light. Next, focus on your family and friends, each one individually, your mother, father, children, mate, brothers and sisters, friends, see a mental image or vision of each one. Finally, reflect on your job, the people in it, what you do and all the other aspects of your life such as hobbies, spiritual practices, etc.

Now, allow yourself to gently float up out of your body. You might either see a vision of this or feel it in some way. As you float up to the center of the room, look down on your body sitting or laying there. Look down and see all the different parts of your personality, your body, your emotions and who you are as a whole person. View your family, your friends, your job and all other aspects of your life. Become aware of how many different pieces and aspects there are to your life, all the multiple parts that God has given to you in life. Now feel the *presence of God* within yourself, the golden thread that ties all these parts together for you in life.

Speak the words aloud (aloud is always more powerful) or silently three times:

O Creator, Reveal To Me How My Life Is Whole, And How I Am At One With You.

Simply listen and be open to any and all experiences you might have. When you feel complete, simply see or feel yourself float back into your body. Now open your eyes and look directly at the burning candle. After a few minutes of focusing on the brightness, allow the brightness to move into your forehead, the seat of your spiritual vision. Continue to focus on the candle as long as feels right to you. Write down your experiences.

Chapter Two

ᘝ

For God So Loved, God Created Love

"My Pure Love Is Within You"

God's LOVE is inside of us all. No one is exempt from the Divine love. God has created all of us to express His living love and we can find God's living love inside of us. Deep within all of us God's love lays like a hidden golden treasure. The key to finding this hidden treasure is to turn inward and seek God's love within our being. Our work here on earth is to love. Our work is to love all that God brings us each moment. God is the truth. There are no other truths.

Love is one of God's greatest gifts to humankind. Although the human consciousness experiences love, the human consciousness does not create love. Love can only be created and given by God. When a person feels love, they feel God. When a person feels God, they feel love.

God is LOVE. God has been called many things by many people, so that today it is often confusing what to know of God. Many words have been used to describe God, and yet God is indescribable for God Is. God Is the feeling of love; Is the feeling of life force flowing within the body; Is the sight of flowers and Is the sound of spring rain; Is the mystical experience of one who prays and fasts in the wilderness; or the mother who bakes bread for her family.

To know God is to know love in the most boundless and expanded state; love with no preconditions, or anticipations; love experienced for the pure glory of loving. For that is what God does every moment; simply loves for the pure ecstasy of loving.

When human beings surrender fear and awareness of self and open to the God consciousness which dwells within them, slowly love creeps into their awareness. Slowly, places open within our being we have kept hidden, slowly like a small creek, which becomes a river, then an ocean. God's love overwhelms and overpowers our being.

The experience of love has been given to humankind as a gift. In some ways humankind has been able to eat its cake and have it too. We have been able to feel the separateness of our form and yet also feel deep love where only Oneness and connection exist. Some people know not of the glory of feeling love. For others, in one moment they feel love for one who is close to them and in the next they choose to separate and choose anger or hate. And yet there is a difference between love and LOVE. LOVE is full God realized consciousness, while love is what we experience in our present state of human consciousness.

It is important to know, for those of us who are committed to our spiritual journey, that love is only just cracking the door. To fully open the door and to walk into God consciousness would be to experience LOVE and full God realization. We, as humankind, must remember that love has been given as a gift from the Creator to show the way. Love is the wayshower, as the Spirit of Christ was living LOVE within the body of Jesus.

Whenever in our lives we choose to feel love, to give love, to open and receive love, to act in a loving way, then we draw our awareness nearer to God consciousness. Whenever we choose to express anger towards our fellow man or woman, we stop ourselves from expressing or receiving love.

Or, if we choose to not open and receive love from another, then we draw away from God and into separateness and fear.

God made manifest in all God's glory and truth on this earth plane is love. Love is both the substance and form of God. God lives in a state of total rapture, for God Is a state of total rapture. All humans, too, can enter into the state of full God realization and rapture.

Entering the state of full God realization is done moment to moment, every moment of our lives. Every moment we choose either God or separateness. We can be one with God in love or be separate from God in our expression towards others of anger, fear, hate, righteousness, jealousy or resentment.

From love flows all of the endearments which we practice with abandon such as kindness, caring, gentleness, softness, openness. Likewise, from lack of love or separateness flows all of the experiences which enmesh us in our separateness such as anger, hate, fear. The absence of love, the closing off from love, is the separation from the Oneness, and in the separation, all acts which humanity deems are inhumane become humanly possible.

God consciousness does not exist in the human consciousness when humans commit murder, wage war, do violence in body, mind, or spirit. Separateness from love, from God, is what spawns these atrocities. And yet God in LOVE does not withdraw the vital life force. At these times, the human heart continues to beat, whether in the breast of a saint or a murderer. God, out of love, does not withhold Her love or withdraw from His creation.

There are many reasons why we choose not to love in any moment. Most of them revolve around fear. Only in choosing fear can we choose a state of non-love. Mostly it is our individual ego's attachment to itself which becomes more important to us than loving. For loving is a blending, a merging; there is no merging in ego's separate view of itself.

Ego holds a separate view of itself out of a deep fear of merging, for in a merging, ego disappears, dies. This deep fear of ego death within the human consciousness continually creates and draws to each of us experiences of pain and fear. Only by looking deep within our individual human consciousness can we begin to see this deep fear.

God creates love and when we experience love, we leave space for the Creator to come into our being. For if that space was not there, the Creator would not be creating the experience of love for you. Every time you feel the experience of love, know God is touching your being directly.

Love is the candle of God which shines brightly in our dark inner world of fear, ignorance, and confusion. If you want to see the people closest to God, see the most loving people. The candles that shine the brightest are those that experience, and hence express, the most love. No matter how fearful the fear or dark the darkness that surrounds them, they continue to experience and express love. Love is the ultimate gift and the ultimate challenge to humankind. No higher state exists on earth than love. It is the state of unbridled joy. No greater challenge has been given to humankind than for us to choose this state of love.

It is the next step forward for humankind. The first

step is an individual one, for each person to commit to experiencing love each moment, no matter what occurs in their life; no matter who attacks them or who takes from them or forces upon them; no matter the darkness, hate, confusion that swirls around them. When a person chooses love and commits to stay in love, a bright candle shines forth in the world. When a group of people do this, a great light shines forth in the world. When a larger group of people do this, a great light shines forth to the stars, when a whole planet does this, a miracle will happen and collective unconscious will become the collective conscious, composed entirely of God's love.

The greatest gift we can give another person is to feel God within ourselves, for from that feeling of oneness with the Creator will flow peace, joy, happiness, love. By feeling full of God within, the fullness and wholeness of God will express from us in every word, gesture, expression.

The journey of expressing God starts with us, deep within our being. It begins, perhaps, with the thought, "God is within me"; or an image of light, or even a point of light which exists within ourselves, or a sense of God speaking from within our being. Just one small crack, one small opening is all it takes for God's awareness to manifest within ourselves. From that beginning point the experience of Divine love begins to grow, as if God has planted a seed of light within the soil of our soul.

This seed of light and love must be nurtured by you, the gardener. You are God's gardener here on earth. God is the master gardener of the Universe. God has planted a holy seed of light within your personal *inner world*. You are to take care of this seed and the soil it has been planted in. You nurture this seed of light by how you take care of your body, by what you eat, by the loving, nurturing relationships and friends you surround yourself with, by what you do for a living and by how supportive your work and home environment is for you, as well as the thoughts and the emotions you choose. By *turning inward* and opening to God's love in our lives, no matter how harsh, difficult or trying our lives are, we open to bringing love into our harshness and difficulty. In bringing love in, we water our soil and nourish the seed of light that God has planted within each of us.

By *turning inward* and seeking God's love, we empower this holy place within our being and create an *inner atmosphere* for it to grow and thrive. As we continually nourish this seed of God's love and light that exists within ourselves with loving relationships, a loving lifestyle, loving friends, loving food, loving activities, it is as if we are putting rich organic natural fertilizer on it, and it begins to grow and build within us.

Soon this seed of light has begun to germinate and to sprout forth from its seed kernel. After awhile the seed breaks ground and a tender, beautiful shoot emerges. This is a Divine shoot that begins to emerge from us, from deep within our being. We do not know what tree this shoot will become yet or even what fruit it will bear. All we know is that God has planted it within ourselves and somehow it is growing upward. We also know that we are providing necessary soil and water for it to grow within us here on earth. We are helping God grow God awareness within ourselves.

This shoot, as it leaves the ground, is very tender and very sweet. It is a real experience and direct revelation of our God connection. And yet it is not a weathered, strong two-hundred-year-old tree, it is a tiny shoot that must be nurtured into full God bloom. Again, we are God's gardeners. We are here to assist God in this growth within ourselves, so we must protect this tender shoot from harshness, from another person stepping on it, either out of ignorance or malice. We must keep the sacred knowledge of this tender beautiful shoot of God expression that has begun to grow within us. Other people may or may not delight in it, but we do. We celebrate the birth of God within ourselves, the birth of Divine love that God has sent.

We begin to meet other people who also have an awareness of this Divine shoot that exists within them and we share our awareness in tenderness and innocence. In this sacred sharing, the shoot begins to grow stronger for it sees its reflection. And so the process is one of nurturing and loving this shoot of light that has begun to grow within our heart. We monitor it, we watch it get stronger, we see it grow higher, we notice the first flower blossom and wonder what type of fruit it will bear, what new life or lifestyle it will create for us. Is it an apple tree, a cherry tree, perhaps something more exotic?

As this tree of God grows within us, it becomes more visible, for it has become too large to hide from the world any longer. At that point there is no need to hide it from the world for it has grown strong enough to withstand the storms of life. And yet no matter how big and powerful this tree becomes, it still must be watered, it still must have soil to grow in, the sun must still shine on it. We still must tend the garden of the tree that has grown from the seed of light that God has planted deep within our being. As we become that tree, we become God's plan for our life, for we have nurtured God within ourselves and God has grown within us. What we have become is what God has chosen for us, and God has chosen our highest expression, our most divine manifestation here in this lifetime.

Whatever we have chosen for ourselves, whatever life our parents have offered us, all that is let go. The only thing that matters at this point is living God's life, loving God's love, doing God's work, being fully attuned to the sacred vibration that exists within each of us. God is always growing within us, God is always being within us. Our work is to open our human consciousness to this tremendous light and love God has placed deep inside each of us. We must seek God's love within our being and we must make God's love more important than anything else in our lives.

The following meditation will assist you to discover that God's love is within you and has already been given. All you need to do is turn within and begin to open to this greatest of gifts.

"My Pure Love Is Within You"

MEDITATION ON DISCOVERING GOD'S LOVE WITHIN

INTENT

Love is God's greatest gift. Although we may drink from the spring of Divine love, we cannot create the spring itself. Love can only be created and given by God. To receive God's love we must *turn inward* and meditate on our own holy place of love. This meditation will help you find your own holy place within.

SUGGESTED ENVIRONMENT

This meditation should be done sitting (sitting is best for all meditations) in the most loving environment you know how to experience. It could be done sitting in nature if this is where you feel nurtured, or in a church, or sitting silently in front of a fire as you are being held by one who loves you; wherever you feel most loved and nurtured. If nothing comes to mind, then simply let your mind wander until something comes in, perhaps something you have never done but have always felt it would be wonderful to do. Also ensure it is a place where you will not be interrupted or distracted, and write your experiences down in a journal.

HOW TO BEGIN

Begin with the following steps:

ᴥ First, find a comfortable position where your spine can be straight, either in a comfortable chair or lying on the floor.

ᴥ Second, close your eyes and do some simple deep breathing for a few minutes, releasing everything that has occurred previously in the day. The deep breathing is very important.

ᴥ Third, adopt an open, meditative attitude by simply reaffirming to yourself that you are open and listening to God.

    ❧ Fourth, focus your attention on the moment and become aware of your breathing and your body.

THE MEDITATION

With your eyes still closed, allow yourself to feel your body. Feel the weight of your body pressing down on the chair you are sitting on. Allow yourself to float gently upward out of your body to the center of the room you are in. Look down on yourself and the surrounding area and realize you have just left your body. Allow yourself to float outside, higher and higher until you can get a good view of the brilliant sun shining down on you. Now focus on this radiant sun that God has created and feel its warmth, light and love. Now allow yourself to see an image of Jesus Christ, the Son of God, in the sun, radiating His love and light upon you personally, and feel His love come directly into your heart.

Now ask the following question aloud or silently three times:

"Creator, How Can I Feel The Unlimited Power Of Your Love In My Life Every Moment?"

Now simply listen for the answer within you. Be open to all your experiences. Allow yourself to saturate yourself in God's Love.

When you feel complete, simply see or feel yourself float back into your body. Write down your experiences. Go about your business for the rest of the day, retaining some feeling of your experience with God's deep Love within you. Try and do this meditation as often as you can. There can never be too much love in your life.

Chapter Three

The Earthly Delight
"My Earth Is Holy"

*T*he earth is God's playground and it is God's original church. We must respect this holy church which God has created for all of us. We must remember we are like children playing on a playground of absolute sacredness. All the birds are holy, all the animals are holy, all that swim in the sea are holy, all that fly in the air, all that walk on the earth.

God is both our Divine Father and our Divine Mother and out of love has created our Holy earthly mother to sustain and nourish us. The mother earth is a holy vessel of love just as you are. Your sacred body and the sacred body of the earth have a sacred connection in God. Open to this sacred connection and your body will learn how to heal and nourish itself. Heal yourself and the earth will heal through you.

The earth is a vibrating force of love, within a sea of infinite bliss. The earth's consciousness and that of the Creator are fully in tune, they are One. The earthly garden is truly a delight, and one of humankind's most important responsibilities is to shepherd, to steward the earthly treasures. Humankind has been given the task of stewardship.

Everything of the earth has a consciousness which is centered in the Oneness. Even humankind, in spite of its human self–awareness, has this God consciousness, it simply denies it through its fear–based ego self. The earth is a living organism which has been created, or evolved, out of the God consciousness. The earth is also a spiritual path for knowing and becoming one with God consciousness.

The purpose of the earth is to teach the human consciousness on its journey to God consciousness about loving connection to all aspects of life. The earth creates an unlimited garden of opportunity for loving connection and feeling a part of the trees, the sky, the animals, the insects, the wind, the rocks, and on and on. Whether it is to our loved ones, our friends, the trees, the oceans, or whatever, we are constantly given opportunities to lovingly connect and to become part of this One great whole. This One whole earth where God shines through every pine needle and every blade of grass and all its different aspects are teaching devices for the individual human psyche on its journey toward God consciousness. The experience of this sacred relationship which all living and nonliving things have together is at the heart of humankind's purpose on the earth.

The time has come for humankind to open to humankind's sacred relationship with the earth by opening to the earth itself in full love. It is time now to integrate all the sacred spiritual teachings of the planet into one whole.

It is time to bring the teachings of the love of Christ and the teachings of the love of the earth together into One circle.

Some must learn how to love Christ and their fellow human beings as much as they love the sacred earth. Some must learn how to love the sacred earth as much as they love the Christ. Many must learn how to love the Christ, the earth and their fellow human beings as much as they love themselves.

The earth is a sacred holy vessel that radiates unceasing love, guidance and healing energy from Her core and from every rock, tree, gust of wind that is created upon Her. The earth is the original church that was created for humankind; the original place where God has asked humankind to worship.

The church of earth is where Jesus worshiped alone in the desert. It is the church where He chose to preach, heal and worship. Earth is where all the saints and great masters went to hear God's voice. Jesus Christ loved the earth. We must learn to love the earth as Christ loved Her. We must learn to love the flowers and all the trees as Christ loved them. We must learn to love all the animals and life as Christ loved them.

The earth is God's most beautiful cathedral, where, if one is quiet and empty, God's voice will speak surely and clearly to us. Nature is God's creation and it is where the human heart can be opened by the Oneness, just by being there. Simply to sit in meditation in the desert, in the mountains, under a tree, or just sitting on the ground is to place one's consciousness in direct physical connection to the earth mother's healing energy. This healing energy radiates out through the earth, through every rock, leaf and blade of grass. To experience this healing energy of the earth is a gift from God.

To place oneself in nature is to place oneself within God's most abundant creation. Within nature, miracles can happen and great healing can occur. In nature, God sings lullabies to us in the joyous songs of the birds, in the gentle rhythm of crickets, in the soft rustling of a breeze. In nature, God displays awesome power in earthquakes, volcanic eruptions, hurricanes. The lullaby of the Divine Mother and the awesome power of the Divine Father exist as One in nature, as they do within each human soul.

It is in nature that we can find great healing energy which can assist us with our own individual healing. A high alpine meadow, a sunny spot by a pond, a solitary path in the trees, all have the potential of transporting us to God to love for they are God's creation. By opening up to the healing power of God in nature, we open up to great nurturing here on earth for our physical and emotional bodies.

To create a garden and work in the soil with our hands and hearts and minds, turning the soil and nurturing it, is in turn to be nurtured by it, allowing it to sift our emotions, clearing and healing them. To allow ourselves to be God's instruments, planting and nurturing seeds from which springs forth life and creation, is in turn to allow ourselves to have new life spring forth within ourselves. At some point in this process of outward gardening we realize there is an inner gardening going on where we have become the garden and God has become the gardener.

The earth offers countless opportunities for this sacred blending with God. Countless opportunities for forming a mystical relationship with the great Mystery, for feeling at one with the Creator. God dwells within the physical reality of earth. One must look beyond the form to the God within.

The earth is always healing herself, and by simply going out into nature, we become part of that natural healing experience for we are all part of the earth. The earth's natural healing energy is always available to support our journey through life. The earth will heal itself fully when each individual comes to know their own light within and walks in balance in their life. For as we heal, the earth heals through us and as the earth heals we will heal, individually and collectively. For humankind to attempt some outward manifestation of healing the earth from a place of fear and anxiety will not heal, only change an outward aspect and not necessarily for the better.

When we act from fear, we create fear, no matter how good our intention. When we act from love, no matter how small our action, we allow the loving power of the Creator to work through us, often creating an impact far greater than our action. The issue for all is to feel our own balance, our center, our light within and to feel how our center connects to the center of the earth. To ground ourselves in the earth and our holy light within so that we may stay in our center, though storms rage around us, we are One with the peace of the Creator within our being.

Go into the wilderness, the deserts, the mountains, the parks, the natural areas of the earth and commune with the Creator in His holy church. Go as if you were one of the ancient prophets or the Master Himself who went there to fast and pray and to commune with the Father directly. So, too, should you seek the solitude and quiet of nature so you may open your heart and hear the still small voice of God within and feel the healing energy of the earth.

The following meditation will assist you to open to the earth's natural healing energy so that you may draw it into your physical body and be renewed and restored by it. The earth loves you very deeply and all you need to do is to spend time and open and receive Her love.

"My Earth Is Holy"

MEDITATION ON OPENING TO THE NATURAL HEALING ENERGY OF THE EARTH

INTENT

The earth's consciousness and that of the Creator are fully in tune. Attuning ourselves to the earth's natural lov-ing energy will tune us to the Creator. This meditation will assist you in becoming attuned to earth's love and thus the love of the Creator.

SUGGESTED ENVIRONMENT

The meditation should be done out in nature. Go out into nature and find a place where you feel nurtured, a place that draws you and a place where you love to be. Especially use this meditation when you are on vacation, connecting to the earth in new locations. The National Parks are a wonderful place to experience the sacredness of the earth, and they are sacred and holy locations. Listen to the natural sounds: the birds, the ocean, the wind, the rustle of trees. Listen to the music of earth as you do this meditation. Also, make sure if doing the meditation alone that you are in a place where you will not be interrupted or distracted.

HOW TO BEGIN

Begin with the following steps:

❧ First, find a comfortable position where your spine can be straight, preferably on the ground where your body is in direct contact with the earth.

❧ Second, close your eyes and do some simple deep breathing for a few minutes.

❧ Third, adopt an open, meditative attitude by simply reaffirming to yourself that you are open and listening to God.

❧ Fourth, focus your attention on the moment and quiet any lingering thoughts. Just become aware of your breathing and your body. Begin to repeat the following affirmation (or one of your own) to yourself silently: "I Am Open To Feeling The Natural Healing Energy Of The Sacred

Earth Which God Has Created"; or focus on a beautiful nature scene in your mind.

THE MEDITATION

Start with your eyes closed and while sitting on the ground, simply allow yourself to feel a vibration in your body coming from deep within your being. Now open your awareness to the earth under your body and begin to feel the deep vibration that is occurring in the earth also. Now allow yourself to feel your body's vibration as an extension of the earth's vibration and vice versa. Now just feel the one vibration which you and the earth are sharing.

Now speak the following aloud or silently three times:

"I Love You Holy Mother Earth, Please Teach Me How To Nourish And Heal Myself In This Lifetime."

Remember, you are addressing God consciousness, which dwells within and creates all form. Do this meditation at least once a week and honor the guidance you receive. Start and end each week with this meditation, perhaps even each day if you feel so guided. You can do this meditation alone or with one or more kindred souls in silence and then afterwards share your experience with one another. Keep a journal handy in which to write down your experiences, visions and feelings.

Chapter Four

❦

World Without End
"I Have A Personal Message For You"

*I*t is by going deep within ourselves that we can experience a personal vision from God. It is by turning our personal lives over to God that we can know and live God's vision, and it is by opening our heart fully to God and trusting God above all else that we will create safety within ourselves to live God's vision.

This is a transition time on the planet for us, personally as well as collectively. We are transitioning from our vision of our lives to God's vision of our lives, personally as well as collectively. Transition times can be full of upheavals because the old is ending and the new is not fully formed and in place and yet, if we can focus on our inner light, we will be transformed as easily as a caterpillar is transformed into a butterfly when the time is right.

We can personally prepare most eloquently for this transition by opening our hearts to God and by *letting go and letting God.* It is *God's process* and *God's process* alone that will lead us from our personal misery and darkness to the light. It is God alone that can put the many diverse pieces of ourselves together into a coherent new whole. It is God alone that can cause all the different spiritual truths that are contained in all the different religions and pieces of humankind to come together in love, into one integrated whole.

Every part of humankind which has sought God consciousness has been given a part of the truth. It is only in integrating these different parts of the truth that the whole will be revealed to humankind. It is only in seeing beyond the individual pieces that humankind will expand toward the Oneness and God consciousness.

Thus, God in infinite wisdom has created a gigantic crossword puzzle, a crossword puzzle of many different spiritual truths. To give any one piece of humankind the whole truth would have created the human behavior of control, domination, and manipulation of those parts of humankind which were not given the whole truth. The human consciousness is not far enough along towards God consciousness to be simply given the whole.

Thus, all the world's religions, all the world's scientists, all the world's organizations, all the world's people have been given a part of the truth, a part of the whole truth. When humankind comes together in brotherhood and sisterhood of love to share their sacred truth, and each aspect is recognized and honored and respected for what it has to contribute, then truly there will be a great explosion of love and light and God consciousness will reveal the whole truth to all equally. It is Christ that can show us how to love one another.

Presently, humankind is drifting toward its ultimate destiny. It is important now for humankind to be aware of its choices. It is time for individuals on the planet to choose their direction either towards Oneness with God consciousness, with all plants and animals, with the overall earth, and especially with each other, or towards more separation and more fear. It is time for all to connect with all. It is simply time for each human soul to choose its destiny.

As the great cleansing occurs on the earth plane now and in the future, and the physical systems, belief systems and other systems that we have come to depend on are transformed, there will only be one place to turn to through the changes and that is directly to God within. In turning within we must also realize that God is within all, and so works through all people in our lives. We must never feel we have a monopoly on God.

Eventually, all of us must get to a place where we trust God fully and completely for all our needs and wants. By leading a fully spiritualized life, we offer our lives to God and ask for healing, love and wholeness. We go with consciousness and intent to the highest part of what we are, and in that process we allow the highest of the high to lead us to where we merge fully.

Humankind has asked to go higher, has asked to bring greater knowledge of life and reality into its human consciousness. God has also committed to take humankind higher and to bring it closer to God in this lifetime. In many ways this lifetime is like a party, a great God party, a true festival of light. Many souls have come here for the great cleansing. There is much power on the planet now, much spiritual power that can be used for movement towards Love consciousness. Likewise, great power exists for going deep into fear if a soul so chooses.

Notice how quickly our lessons are coming now in life. Notice how quickly the unkind word we speak or action we take comes back to us in some life lesson. Notice how quickly the anger we target on another comes roaring back, or the hate or the envy or the jealousy. Whatever we give out will come back to us; so as we sow, we shall reap; this is God's law. It's just that now the lessons happen so quickly, they are so obvious, so abundant. It is time to live our spirituality. It is time to treat others as we would have them treat us.

These lessons are God's gift to us now. We have said we want to be closer to God, we have said we want to bring light to all of our dark parts, we have said we want to open our hearts and our lives to the Christ consciousness. We have said we want wholeness and integration in our lives, and so it is provided, quickly and with great power in these times.

We simply must open to these lessons for they have the potential, depending on our openness, of moving us to a very high place in this lifetime. As great spiritual power is now on the earth moving intimately in our personal individual life, so is this great power moving in the collective human consciousness. This great power on the earth now can be used either creatively or destructively. It is an individual choice.

What we try to destroy outside ourselves will eventually come back in some form to destroy us. What we try to bring love and light to outside of ourselves will eventually bring love and light back to us in some form. A level of connection and wholeness is developing on the planet now that has never existed in the past, and along with this level of connection must come a greater awareness of the consequence of any one action.

As you view international events and worldly happenings, examine your own life for similar patterns. For international happenings are but symbolic occurrences of that which is occurring within each individual human consciousness and all human life. The transformation of eastern European countries from totalitarian restrictive government to a state of more open and less restrictive government is an example of the transforming collective energy of human consciousness. Transmuting the restrictive energy of individuals and collective consciousness is the outward manifestation of a deep inward process which is going on individually and collectively.

Likewise, if the eastern European governments would have resisted the evolution, a much harsher outcome could have occurred. There is a great transforming energy that is moving on the planet now, seeking to move the earth and the human species upward in consciousness as well as in each of us personally. Resisting this great transforming energy will bring each of us and our collective species very difficult times. Opening to this transforming energy will bring rebirth, transformation, a new life, a new perspective.

The earth will not be destroyed by this great cleansing that is occurring, but it will be changed and it will be cleansed. Our souls will not be destroyed by this great cleansing, but they will be purified and transformed. Our human lives may or may not be taken, but either way they, too, will be changed and transformed. If we elect to grow towards our inner light, the light of God taking Christ's hand in ours, then how we remain on the planet will be very different than today. Our inner experience of life will be very God connected and God centered.

The laws of God will not be written in books; they will be written in our individual hearts so that our actions and words will manifest our higher selves. The light of God will be felt within ourself and will be visible in all our brothers and sisters. Life will become a humble and simple experience and humble exercise in doing God's work and fully opening to the Christ consciousness within. Life will become a giving away experience rather than a taking or accumulating experience, for the balance of light and dark within ourselves will have shifted. Our lives will become ones of love and creation and not destruction and domination. For we will know that there is only God and God does not dominate, God only loves; and so we will not seek to dominate or force our fellow man, woman, or any animal, only to love them.

God consciousness has imbued every individual piece of every relationship, every group with an aspect of the spiritual truth. No one human soul has ever been given the whole, and yet there have been souls that have fully expanded into full God realization, and the living Christ Spirit is the wayshower. The giving of only parts of the truth are intended for the human consciousness as a teaching device so it can join together in wholeness and integration to share the truth. When an individual soul approaches and realizes full God consciousness, that soul opens to the whole truth.

It is integration with God consciousness and wholeness that humankind cries out for and yet integration and wholeness is what humankind resists the most. Resistance to spiritual truth and God consciousness is epidemic in humankind. Humankind hears many different voices speaking to it. Some voices inspire human souls towards God consciousness. Other voices, the voices of fear, seek to deepen resistance to Oneness.

Part of the confusion of the human psyche is not understanding that when we listen outside of ourself with our human ears, we will never know if we are hearing God speaking for God or man speaking for God. However, if man or woman were to focus within themselves to hear the Creator's voice and to feel the Presence of God, he or she would be sure to only hear God, no matter who was speaking to them. Deep within each human soul lies a direct connection to Oneness, to the God consciousness. When man or woman focus on hearing God within themselves, only one voice can speak to him or her, that of the Creator.

And yet even by focusing within, the sacred voice can be confusing. It is not the sacred voice that is in confusion, it is the human being, the human receptor that creates static. God consciousness speaks to every human soul from within directly. It is the God-given right of every human soul to hear the sacred voice directly and intimately within their entire being. To the extent that the human beingness is churning with fear, with anger, with hate, with confusion, then in a sense this will create a static, similar to a radio channel.

Within this static, the sacred voice is still speaking fresh and clear as a mountain stream, but it is not being clearly heard over other noise. It is as if the sacred voice speaks to us, but the moment we feel fear, the words are missed or separation speaks or places other words there. So in the end the message does not always come through wholly. That is, our personal static can confuse the clear message of the sacred voice within each of us. Which is why we must do our individual emotional, physical and mental healing work now emptying out all of our personal static.

It is as if God consciousness is a great radio transmitter broadcasting to all the Universe and every part of the Universe, from a human being, to an ant, to a tree, to a rock, to the stars, which contains within it a radio receiver tuned only to this God frequency. God speaks to all parts, continuously and universally. Because God speaks directly to us, God always speaks in a manner that is right for us individually. For one person it is words, for another it is feelings, for yet another it is intuition. God knows all and God knows how to speak to all.

To hear the sacred voice within most clearly will mean

a commitment for each of us individually to purify our physical bodies, to purify our emotional states, to purify our mental state, and to seek love above all. With purification of these different parts of ourselves, the sacred voice within will be heard clearly and distinctly, with no static, and we will be clear channels of love.

Now is the time for all of us to purify our bodies through appropriate vegetarianism, drinking quantities of pure water, regular exercise, breathing, and aloneness complemented with equal amounts of time of being together with people, for this will make our bodies and our consciousness ready for hearing God's voice. These things do not in and of themselves bring us to God; they simply prepare our physical/emotional vehicle so we may feel, hear, and see God clearly. Now is the time for all of us to purify our emotions by maintaining a constant focus on love, for this will make our emotions ready for experiencing God's love. Now is the time for all of us to purify our minds through stillness and meditation, for that will make our mind ready to receive God's wisdom. Now is the time for all of us to integrate our lives by constantly being aware of the Creator speaking to us, for that will make us ready to receive God fully, directly, wholly into our lives. Now is a time of preparation for this great wholeness that is available in this lifetime to each of us.

The new age, as it is referred to, is about God calling; God consciousness putting out a call to all human beings on our planet. It is as if a person has a radio perched upon their refrigerator as a decoration and has not used it for twenty years. All of a sudden one day we walk by and static is coming out of the radio. We are surprised, the radio is not supposed to work, it never has before, and we wonder what mystery is at work here. We also realize that everyone has a similar radio within their homes and all the radios are beginning to broadcast. And we also realize that very soon God consciousness will be speaking to each of us directly, advising us as to the path we are to take individually, moving us toward Oneness and away from separation.

In any situation or interaction there must be space for the Creator to speak. By choosing love, gentleness, caring, we create that space. By choosing hate, anger, fear, we close that space. One choice creates space, one choice destroys space.

Only by choosing love can we experience love. Only by remembering that God's love lives in our hearts every moment can we have the *inner strength* to choose love in times of persecution, humiliation, or when we are the target of another's anger or fear. It is only by committing ourselves to staying in a place of love that we will be able to avoid going into our intellect to explain our love and thereby leaving it. We must always remember we alone can choose to leave our experience, no one chooses for us; we are fully responsible for our choice.

Truth does not come from the mind, truth comes through our hearts. We must still the mind so the heart can speak to it, for all the heart knows is love, and love is the only truth. Truth is never cruel, truth is always loving, for truth is love. Remember, in spite of the world, love; because of the world, love; to answer the world, love; to question the world, love.

A definition of wholeness is to acknowledge it is God's love and the light that is the guiding force in our lives, with all other aspects of our life supporting this. It is the love and the light that is guiding us to wholeness and integration, using all circumstances of our life to accomplish this. The single most comforting action or step that we can take for our earthly selves is to open our hearts in love and listen to the still small voice of God within. It is our lifeline to Consciousness. It is a way to understand, to know.

Now is the time to take full responsibility for our lives and to take full accountability for all aspects of our lives. We are, at our core, spiritual beings; spiritual beings having a human experience, for reasons only known to the Creator. In our human experience the Creator has an individual relationship with each of us and we are sovereign in that relationship.

It is time to own all of our emotions that need clearing and that are buried deep within us. It is erroneous to view other people as causing us anger, grief, or hurt. Other people are simply catalysts to unlock our fears. And while it is true we may be attacked by another person's emotional unconsciousness, our emotional reaction has to do with us and not the other person's attack.

Emotions can be expressed as clearing emotions. Clearing emotions are those that allow us to let go of our unconsciousness, allowing God's love to replace the area where we were holding on to them. This is personal accountability. Emotions that are expressed and targeted at an object or a person are toxic emotions. Toxic emotions are those that take us deeper into our unconsciousness making it difficult to let God's love and light in. This is not personal accountability.

The core issues that we work on in our lives are always the places we are most resistant to God. Indeed, they are the places we spend our whole lives working on letting God in. To heal and to bring the light into our most contracted and resistant places is the major reason we are alive. The areas that are not working in our lives are in need of observation. Not obsessing or focusing or gossiping or projecting or blaming, just simply observing, witnessing. Life brings to us those experiences that are necessary for us to move forward.

We attract those experiences that will reflect back to us our greatest fears, the fears which may be so deeply rooted within us that we have no sense they exist within. Thus, only through the clarity of a worldly experience, outside of ourselves, is it brought to our attention. Mostly we push these experiences away or blame them on someone or something, as they are too painful for us.

These experiences are reminders from a very loving God who supports our slow, feeble steps towards light and love. Always the light or darkness within us creates the light or darkness outside of ourselves in the form of life experiences. Obsessing and focusing on these experiences does not necessarily serve our journey to wholeness. Especially if our focusing leads us further away from looking within.

Everything which occurs in our life, from the darkest of experiences to the most loving of experiences, is meant to bring our focus inward on God. Once we begin to see our light within we will see others' light within, irrelevant of whether our human experiences are pleasant or unpleasant. It is by first focusing on the incredible love, joy and light that exist within ourselves that we can begin to let go of our positive and negative human experiences.

The journey to wholeness is one of trust, for when we are in the middle of an unpleasant experience it is important to trust God. No matter how unpleasant and miserable the experience that is brought to our doorstep, we must go through our fears, our misery, our anger, our hate, with complete trust in God, looking for God's light, listening for God's still small voice.

As we go through our fears deeply, with commitment, in openness, trusting God to lead us to wholeness, the miraculous occurs in our life. What once seemed so awful becomes transformed, as from a caterpillar to a butterfly. What once seemed so hopeless has simply become the raw material for the transformation; the next step for the higher step in our lives.

Attachment to outcomes is one of the major ways we stumble on our journey to wholeness. In our attachment we either resist the message that is being communicated to us or even worse, we deny the experience that is occurring. The river of life has a very strong, fast, true current. A current so clear that it propels us on our journey in spite of our resistance or our lack of awareness of its force upon us.

When we attach ourselves to an outcome we make a decision on how we wish the river to be. In a sense we say to God: "God, be this way." We may attach ourselves all we like and yet how can a twig caught in the strong current of a mighty river ask the river to change its course? It is only in thinking the twig is separate from the river that the question can even be asked. The twig and the river are One; even with the illusion of a separate twig and river, they are still One; the river is guiding the twig, in a sense unseen and unheard and yet obviously.

In our striving towards wholeness we may try many paths. All paths lead to the one true path and that is the path of emptiness. By embracing emptiness, we empty ourselves of our human good, bad, misery, preconceptions, whatever. In that place of emptiness, wholeness exists within us, for the experience of wholeness is the experience of God. To experience Oneness with the Mystery, with the Creator who dwells within all of us, is to experience wholeness.

Wholeness means emptiness. A whole person is an empty person. A whole relationship is an empty relationship. A whole experience is an empty experience. Relationships that are filled are not whole. A person that is filled is not whole. Wholeness does not come from integrating one's life, although it is a by-product. Wholeness comes from emptying out one's life. To empty out can mean to give away and giving away may not mean emptying out.

If you wish to be whole, every day, empty yourself

out, and in that empty space within you God will work. Then you will experience wholeness, there is no other way. And yet each person must hear these words within himself or herself for their truth to be absorbed. All of us are seeking our highest level of wholeness and integration at any moment. That wholeness can be very elusive when we depend solely upon our own human skills, life experiences, thoughts, and feelings.

As human beings, we are composed of many parts: some clarity, some confusion, some centeredness, some ungroundedness, some love, some non-love in whatever form it takes. It is this package of ourselves that we have co-created with God. We bump and grind our way through life with our sense of what we should or shouldn't be doing, our understanding of why events occur or don't occur, our lack of knowing and understanding. As a human being we do the best we can with any situation. And many situations leave us feeling absolutely awful about life, as if we have been flattened by a steam roller.

Driving through life without an awareness of the Creator within ourselves, without some sense of our inner love and sacred connection, makes for a harsh life and harsh experiences. Only in opening to the Creator's love within ourselves, to the Christ light within, does the world and our earthly experiences begin to soften and mellow for us. As we feel the love within, so it is manifested in the outside world in the creation of our lives and in their eventual transformation.

As we shut ourselves off from the love within ourselves, so is its lack manifested in our lives and reflected back to us. As we open to love more fully, more consistently with commitment, the deeper we go into our relationship with the Creator. To go to our place of love within is to go to our sacred relationship within. To go to love within is to create love without, in our earthly lives.

It is difficult to go to a place of love when anger or negativity is being focused on us. It is difficult to go to inner love when someone is judging us, or attempting to control us, or editing our behavior in some way; or when we are dying in some way. And this is the place we must go to for this is the place of wholeness and integration that exists within us. It is the place of grace that God has given to us, no matter what the vagaries of the world bring to us.

If we are attacked or criticized, so be it; give the form away, in that moment. If we give our form away, as we must anyway some day, and simply reside in our God consciousness, we experience what Spirit experiences, consciousness without form. Remember, deep inside, you are Consciousness first, you are form second.

All our machinations at protection are mental gyrations, for we create suits of emotional armor to protect ourselves from criticism. Once the emotional armor is on, we become trapped in it; it is not protection anymore, it now becomes a jail, a prison. In that jail, the ultimate trap of form, we damage our form and other forms, for blindly we forget we are Consciousness deep within and believe instead we are just form. We close our hearts, to God and to each other, and we suffer from the pain of a closed heart.

By choosing love fully inside in the most awful moment, and in that process releasing all expectations of outcome, we take a giant step forward in our God connection, a giant step forward into our own healing and integration as spiritual, emotional, physical beings. However, we can't deceive God. If we have not fully chosen love inside and empty ourselves of all but love, it will work for us only to the extent of our choice.

There are many aspects to our beingness, including: our spiritual selves, our emotional selves, our physical selves, and our mental selves. Our spiritual aspect always chooses love in the moment, and our emotional, mental, and physical aspects may resist out of fear, ignorance, or illusion. So our emotional issues and unhealed places are manifested in the situation at hand and reflected back to us. Reflected back to us because we are unable to feel and see those unhealed places within us.

It is in many ways the choosing of love that we create our worst outward manifestations. For in the commitment to love, Spirit leads us into our most unhealed and unwhole places. Not to punish us, rather to give us an opportunity to turn our shadows within to the love and the light. And so given that opportunity we either take advantage of it and become fully accountable for it, or we push it away.

In either case, usually we do the best we can. What we often forget is that we don't have to do it alone, by our-selves, as just a human being of mixed results. We can go directly to the Creator within and say, "Please do this one for me God; please take over Lord; please speak through me Lord; please behave through me Lord." We can appeal directly to the *living Christ* which inhabits all our hearts and ask Him to shine His great light so that we can see the truth clearly. We can ask God for help.

Remember this is preparation time, transition time for the coming *Light of God* and the best way to prepare is to open your heart and trust fully in God. Be open to receiv-ing God's vision for your personal life and to God's iden-tity for you rather than one you have built up through the world and which the world has assigned to you. The fol-lowing meditation will assist you to access your deepest inner source of God and to receive a personal message from God.

"I Have A Personal Message For You"

MEDITATION TO RECEIVE A
<u>PERSONAL VISION FROM GOD</u>

INTENT

This meditation will assist you to access your deepest inner source of God and to bring into your conscious awareness God's personal vision for your life. This may be for a specific aspect or for your lifetime or for just one day at a time. This meditation can give you a visual image, or sense or knowingness of what you would look like, feel like, be like, or talk like if you were in perfect attunement with your Creator.

SUGGESTED ENVIRONMENT

This meditation may be performed anywhere at any time, although just after dawn is a powerful time to do it. If doing the meditation alone, ensure it is a place where you will not be interrupted or distracted. Keep a journal handy in which to write down your experiences.

HOW TO BEGIN

Begin with the following steps:

❧ First, find a comfortable sitting position where your spine can be straight.

❧ Second, close your eyes and do some simple deep breathing for a few minutes.

❧ Third, adopt an open, meditative attitude by simply reaffirming to yourself that you are open and listening to God.

❧ Fourth, focus your attention on the moment and quiet any lingering thoughts. Just become aware of your breathing and your body. Begin to repeat the following affirmation (or one of your own) to yourself silently: "I Am Open To Receiving A Personal Message From God," or, "I Commit To Placing My Life Wholly In God's Hands And Trusting God's Process For My Life." If you are a visual person try focusing on an image of a shining white light. When you feel complete with this part begin the following meditation.

THE MEDITATION

With your eyes closed again do some deep rhythmic breathing, releasing all that has happened to you in the day, while focusing on a bright *inner light* within your being. Next allow the light you are seeing or experiencing in some way within yourself to become a *River Of Light*. Just continue to focus on this powerful *River Of Light* that is flowing through you now. Then ask the following question aloud or silently three times:

> *"Please, Creator, Reveal To Me Thine Vision Of My Being, Of My Life With You, And What My Next Step Is?"*

Try and do this meditation at least once a week.

Chapter Five

❦

The Disciples
"I Am Gathering You Together For Me"

*A*ll of humankind belongs to the same spiritual family. All people on the planet are holy, they are all our sacred brothers and sisters. We are all spiritual brothers and sisters at the deepest levels. Even our earthly parents share this brotherhood and sisterhood with us, for our true parents are Divine in origin.

We have all been born into human families, and no matter what our experience, there has been great learning. Some of our human experiences have been loving and nurturing, some have been tragic and painful. The degree of love or fear our parents, our brothers or sisters, or our relatives introduced each of us to in life is irrelevant. It is important to know that the spark of God exists within each of our human parents and siblings no matter how many layers of fear covered that spark or no matter if their love was not covered but shone brightly on us throughout childhood. It is also important to know that we can heal our inner pain, anytime we choose, by releasing it and taking it to our inner light, our place of God within.

Out of our childhood experiences, learning took place, opening of our hearts took place through all the bad and the good. And so it is important to honor our human parents, our human family for all it has brought us. It is important to bless our human family, our parents, and our relatives and to let them go. To give them all to God and to trust the Lord in our giving.

Humankind is one great community of spiritual families, one great brotherhood, one great sisterhood. None of our brothers and sisters are our masters; there are no exceptions. There is only one master and that is God, who dwells within all creation. Some of our brothers and sisters are more open to God than others, but that does not make them our master. It does, however, speak to their personal relationship with God, and thus we can strive to open ourselves to God, more and more, until we, too, have a deep, intimate and loving relationship with our Creator. Thus we can learn from them how to open to God more fully in our own personal lives.

We are all fellow travelers on this God–opening life journey. We are all equal in the spark of God that dwells within us, and it is true that we are all in an upward movement no matter what our life is like. There is a holy light within everyone, within all humanity, which emanates from the core of Being. And this light, this spark of God is subtle, for it comes from another reality, the spiritual reality. To develop an awareness of this subtle holy light within ourselves, to experience it, to see it in others, we must focus on it and we can only do that by going *inside ourselves* or *looking within* others to this other reality, this other world.

Those who are willing to *look within* themselves as well as others to see this holy light will move upward on their life journey with less difficulty than others will. Because of their focus on the light, which emanates from all creation, they will be able to achieve more of what they are meant to achieve in their lifetime.

Today, God's light has begun to bring people together so that they may get to know one another. It is as if the Creator has turned a light on between certain people so that they can see one another and are attracted to being with each other in a new way, in God's way. In coming together in wholly new ways and in spiritual families, we will let go of our human concept of mother and father and cease to look upon other humans as our creators, for there is only one Creator. We will let go of our human mother and father and we will let go of them as the creators and the sustainers of our life.

From then on we will pray for the Creator to bring our spiritual family to us and each of us to our right and per-fect spiritual family. In coming together in this manner we will re-create our childhood as God intended, for we are all children of God. In this re-creation great healing will take place and great knowing of God will occur, for it will be a Divine childhood based fully on the light and love of God.

Gone will be the placing of human consciousness, or human experience, on a higher pedestal over each of us. There will be no control from the human mother or father, for that is of the past and we have given that all to God. What we will have is simple equality of a spiritual brother-hood and sisterhood worshiping the *Light of the Creator* within all creation.

It is true that our human mother, father, or siblings may be in our spiritual families. It is equally true that they may not be. God will bring the appropriate people together and God will pull the inappropriate people apart. Our work is to be open and unattached, to tune in to that deep place of God that exists within each of us and follow God's voice in this process of spiritual gathering.

Today it is time to gather a group of like-minded people together and simply sit and feel God and feel love and feel the Mystery. This will create much space for God's Spirit to come in, for a group of people sitting together feeling God has great power and more love than sitting alone or individually.

God has created the soul, man and woman have created the personality. If man and woman would focus on their inner light, their inner love, their Godself, then it would burst forth like a great explosion. Man and woman focus on the personality and thus focus on the least meaningful part of their being. Only by focusing on a person's true core do we ever really see them.

For someone to say the personality is from God is analogous to saying a shadow on a wall is from a bright light. God is the Light, the personality is the shadow. The shadow is incomparable to the actual Light. Our personalities are so incomparable it is folly to even compare that part of ourselves to God and yet God's light illumines all of our worldly parts.

God burns very brightly within all of us. Most people have covered over their God spark with so many layers of their personality that they are simply not aware of God within them. When God gets so bright within the soul that it pours through a personality so that others can see the light and the personality has awareness within, then a great realization of God has taken place.

In order for this to happen the personality may have to work where it is blind, where it cannot see or feel. Sometimes it must rely simply on faith and trust, and then God will burn through. Most people do not want to work unless they can see a direct reward or an immediate gratification, but humankind is evolving in its God consciousness. It is evolving to a place of the ever-present God within its individual being, its individual manifestation of the One consciousness.

Those who would stand in front of large groups of people and command attention to move people one way or another will become more and more irrelevant. For within each human heart the voice of God will speak directly, spontaneously, every moment, guiding each soul to its absolute highest level of perfection. And in this dialogue, there will be no interest or enthusiasm for the average person to listen to another's human consciousness. It will cease to be anything of value.

All human beings, at this point in their spiritual development, should visualize themselves as disciples of the Lord. In their discipleship they should see their Lord speaking directly to their heart, within themselves. The words God speaks to them from within is the holiest of the holies, the most sacred of the sacred. In choosing to hear and act upon those words spoken directly to us from within, we follow our highest path in this life and we empower God within us.

Full manifestation of God consciousness within us and the emptying out of the human consciousness will bring the experience of Christ consciousness to the soul. The soul yearns for this complete perfect union with God, incarnating in many forms through many lifetimes.

When the temple of the body is empty of human consciousness, the vessel will draw to it the One consciousness. Jesus was one who was completely and perfectly open to the Creator that dwelled within Him. In opening to God fully and experiencing His Christ consciousness, He showed all of us the way, thus He is the wayshower.

The full Christ consciousness is what every soul on earth is here to experience. The life we have chosen and which God creates for us according to our choice is meant to guide us, in the long run, to perfect union with God. All of us are on our path, being led higher and higher through every lifetime. Sometimes our opening to God is great, sometimes it is small. The amount does not matter for the opening always occurs; this is the purpose of life.

All on the earth at this present moment are disciples of the Creator. It is time for humankind to take up this discipleship with the Creator and allow the Creator to teach each human heart directly. Within every human being the sacred voice of God speaks. God is our Master and dwells within us and we are not God, nor is our personality God. If we fall into the delusion that we as personality are God, our lessons will be harsh in order to teach us the truth and likewise if we resist knowing that God is within us, creating us every moment, then we will turn in blindness away from the One source within all.

It is time for all of us to open our hearts to God and know that we need nothing but to open to His still small voice within. To help in hearing God's voice within, many earthly teachers have been sent. A true teacher is one who assists another to go deeply within their being and experience for themselves, firsthand, the realization of God Himself speaking to them.

Now is the time for all of us to reach out to our brothers and sisters on the planet and to let our barriers down with each other. The way to let our barriers down is not through attack, or even clarity, but through love, gentleness and through the understanding of safety and the contentment that is there when all fear is released. Our barriers are let down when we bring them into our inner light so they can be consumed by the light. By drawing all our obstacles in our life into our inner light, they will become transformed by the light and they will become light themselves.

God is bringing like-hearted and like-spirited people together now. The Divine Father/Mother is bringing people together in simple spontaneous gatherings in order to reveal who we are in spiritual families with, and to turn the light on among people so we can discover one another. These are people who will begin to become very important to one another and play central roles in each other's life for each other's spiritual unfolding. God is planting a *spiritual garden* on the planet now and we are all in it.

In planting this *spiritual garden* God knows which people are best suited to be together. There may be people in your life you will need to release back to God. This does not make them wrong or bad or less than or more than. They just belong with others more compatible with their hearts and minds. They belong with people who they can sing in harmony and unison with, just as a great chorus sings together; just as you need to grow and sing with people who have similar hearts and minds to yours.

The following meditation will help you open your heart to your spiritual family. Trust God and simply focus your attention on your love of God and be open to God's plan. Be open to your feelings and your intuition as to whom to reach out to and how to begin offering your heart and your home to people so that your Divine Parents may send the right and perfect people into your lives and into Their gatherings. Now is the time for our spiritual families to begin to come together in God. Open your heart to your spiritual brothers and sisters that God brings into your life. Begin to meet with them and share communion with the light. Begin to pray together and to listen to the still small voice of God together.

"1 Am Gathering You Together For Me"

MEDITATION TO OPEN YOUR HEART TO YOUR SPIRITUAL FAMILY

INTENT

All human beings on the planet are our brothers and sisters. All are kindred souls who at their deepest levels are seeking to bring God fully into their human lives irrelevant to their awareness or level of development. This meditation will assist you to open your heart to your brothers and sisters of light so you can be in touch with another's God essence. By focusing on another's inner love and light you will see their truth.

SUGGESTED ENVIRONMENT

Find a quiet place, a nurturing place, a place that you feel safe in and where you will not be interrupted or distracted. It could be done inside in a quiet, darkened room, with a candle burning to symbolize the coming *Light of God.* Keep a journal handy in which to write down your experiences, visions and feelings so you can review them regularly.

HOW TO BEGIN

Begin with the following steps:

🍂 First, find a comfortable position where your spine can be straight, either in a comfortable chair or lying on the floor.

🍂 Second, close your eyes and do some simple deep breathing, releasing everything that has occurred previously in the day. The deep breathing is very important.

🍂 Third, adopt an open, meditative attitude by simply reaffirming to yourself that you are open and listening to God.

🍂 Fourth, focus your attention on the moment and quiet any lingering thoughts. Just become aware of your breathing and your body. Begin to repeat the following affirmation (or one of your own) to yourself silently: "I Am Opening My Heart To God." If you are a visual person try focusing on an image of a shining white light. When you feel complete with this part begin the following meditation.

THE MEDITATION

With your eyes still closed, begin to see a six pointed star of brilliant white light–the Christ Star–hovering above your body, bathing you in the pure white light of God. Feel or experience the pure Christ Light pouring into your heart, releasing all your fears about being in relationships with people, dissolving all your resistance to people, healing all your wounds with people. Feel the Christ Light making you whole in relationships with people so you can blend with them selflessly in harmony, joy, and love.

Now say the following words out loud or silentlythree times:

"Oh Christ Light, Open My Heart To The Spiritual Brothers And Sisters You Will Guide Into My Life And Me Into Theirs, I Am Ready."

Be open to your experiences and write them down in a journal.

As an additional meditation you could bring up an image or a feeling of the particular person you feel attracted to. As you are seeing them say these words aloud or silentlythree times:

"Creator, Please Reveal Yourself To Me In My Brother Or Sister _____ ." (Say the name.)

Simply stay in a meditative place, open and receptive to what comes.

Chapter Six

❦

The Coming Of The Lord
"I Am the Still Small Voice Within You"

*T*he coming of the *Light of Christ* is signaling a new way for all of humanity to communicate directly with God. In this simple way God's sacred voice can be heard as the still small voice within.

So can each of us, by focusing on communing directly with the Creator of the Universe, hear Him as the still small voice within, guiding us gently on a path of love and light home to Him. It is time for all of us to realize that each can talk directly to God every moment and that God speaks directly to every person. Mostly this dialogue goes on in our unconscious mind, for to be conscious of the dialogue, the following is necessary:

- **LETTING GO OF BUSYNESS**
- **INNER QUIETNESS**
- **STILLNESS**
- **STOPPING THE CHATTER OF THE HUMAN PERSONALITY, MIND, EGO**
- **DETACHMENT FROM ONE'S EMOTIONS**
- **OPENNESS TOWARDS GOD–CHOOSING GOD**

It is by faith and faith alone that each of us can know God intimately and it is by faith that we can learn to trust that the Creator speaks directly to us, guiding us each moment. God knows all, God is all, and God provides all. Never doubt your ability to hear Him speaking directly to your heart.

The title of this chapter is symbolic of the next chapter in humankind's spiritual development. The coming of the Lord is not an event which will happen outside of us, on a global scale, although those types of events will occur. The coming of the Lord will occur in each human heart. The Lord will come directly to each soul and manifest within the heart on this earthly plane. Thus, the choice each of us has to this coming is whether we will open our hearts or not. The Lord cannot come to us unless we are open and receptive to this coming. A closed heart is the surest way to turn our back to God's coming, and it is through listening to the still small voice within that we allow ourselves to be guided on a perfect heart–opening process.

In order to hear the still small voice within we must become very still and very small so that only God's voice echoes through our being. If we are full of our self, our mind is chattering, or our emotions are engaged,we will not be able to hear the still small voice or hear it clearly.

Hearing God's voice clearly is about emptying out our small self so we can hear and experience our larger Self.

Within every human being, a struggle occurs. The struggle is between the God consciousness and the human consciousness. In this struggle are the spiritual lessons each human soul is here to learn. Within each person, deep in his or her being, is the truth of his or her life. No one can know another's full truth of life. No one can know another's full truth for that covenant exists only between the individual soul and the Lord. In the future, the way of God, within oneself, will be the way of the average man rather than the way of the special person such as the saint or the sage.

The planet is moving toward the second coming of Christ and the Light of Christ will be birthed in individual hearts on the planet. Those who have chosen the path of God consciousness and have opened their hearts to all will experience a rapture, a mystical feeling of oneness at a point in the future. This experience of rapture will take place all over the planet in the same moment. It is this deep experience of God that will leave no doubt, in those who experience it, of the birth of Christ consciousness within them.

God will ask only one thing for bestowing this wondrous gift upon us. That is that today, in this very moment, we choose the path of God consciousness and we choose to love God with all our heart, soul, and mind. To love God with all our heart, soul and mind will cause love to flow for all our brothers and sisters on the planet. To love God will cause love to flow for all the rocks, trees, animals on the planet, for the planet itself. To love God with all our heart will cause love to flow for all the stars and planets, and the knowingness that they are all within us and we within them.

Once the human soul has chosen the path of God consciousness, he or she will be given many opportunities to open their human reality more and more to God. To some extent each person will be given spiritual tests to assist them on their journey toward Oneness. These tests are not meant to harm or to blame; they are just opportunities that will be presented, moment to moment, that will allow us, through our choice of loving God, to reduce our separation and to expand our God consciousness.

If in our ignorance–or in our lacking the clarity to follow God's still small voice–we choose wrong, God will continue to give us other opportunities. With every teaching and evolving lesson that comes into our lives, it is simply another opportunity to bring God closer into our hearts and to surrender a little more of our human self. Once we have chosen in our hearts the path of God consciousness, the commitment will have been made. We will then draw into our lives all the divine opportunities necessary to surrender ourselves fully to God consciousness.

We are not to be alone in these spiritual tests, for the God consciousness will guide us through them. As humans, with human consciousness, how can we know what God requires of us, or what is asked of us, or what the Creator's will is? We can't; only God will know. What we are given once we have opened our heart of hearts to the path of God is the ability to hear the sacred voice within, and through this Divine voice we will be told what God's will is for our personal life.

It is in the heat of the moment of the spiritual opportunity that we each must ask, "Thy Will, not my will." In calling forth God consciousness in our hearts we will hear or know or see or feel God's presence and the cause of our action.

Only we will know deep within our hearts and our beings what is the right word or action or behavior that is being asked for by the sacred voice. It is in loving the voice of God consciousness within ourselves and following what we hear that we choose God in the moment, allowing the Creator to guide us home.

There will be many who will come into your life and wish to speak to you of God's voice. This will be confusing. All human souls are to know that they have a direct connection to the God consciousness. All they have to do to hear the sacred voice, is to choose the path of God, to open their heart and love God, and to create quiet time to hear the Master speak to them from within.

There will be no substitute for hearing the sacred voice directly. To want to have God consciousness speak to us through another is to choose separation. Only within our heart of hearts, our deepest being, can we know the voice of truth. There are many teachers that will come, and sacred practices which will be available, to assist and facilitate each human being's ability to hear the sacred voice directly within himself or herself.

There was a time in the development of the human consciousness when humans deemed it appropriate to have others intercede directly to the Mystery for them, to act as go–betweens between God consciousness and human consciousness. The time for any human being to stand between God consciousness and an individual is past, no matter what the reason or purpose or intent. God desires a one–to–one intimate love relationship with everyone on the planet. It is in this intimate, sacred love relationship that the individual separate human being will experience God realization and Christ consciousness.

Although appropriate for a person to assist, to help, or to facilitate another's hearing of the Creator's voice within, it is not appropriate for one person to receive inner guidance for another person. God is not served by our separation from God; and yet methods, teachers, and processes will be there to assist each of us to connect directly within ourselves to God's still small voice.

Deep within each human heart the still small voice of God speaks. Listening to, hearing, and following the still small voice can change our lives. Imagine the possibilities. The truest source of truth, the deepest wisdom, the most abundant love, exists within the open heart of each of us. All we have to do is tune in to God's channel within us, experience it, and let it guide us to God. Station **WGOD** is broadcasting this very moment to you, and the radio receiver was placed in your heart at birth by Divine grace.

No more frantic searching for the parts that are missing outside of ourselves, no more giving away our power to other human beings because we cannot find it within ourselves; only God's voice speaking to each of us individually, in words, images, feelings, knowingness unique to us, in ways only we can understand, soothing us, comforting us, guiding us to a life of greater and greater wholeness each moment.

Once we become aware of God's voice speaking to us, the world always looks a little different. We take a step back from the outside world into the inner world. As we go deeper into our inner world we more clearly experience our true source.

Once our awareness is attuned to this true source within ourselves, we more often ask within what is the right direction for us, or action, or words to speak. Less and less often we rely on advice or judgment from outside ourselves, from friends or relatives or from our sense of what would be popular or unpopular, or acceptable or unacceptable.

As we slowly begin to make our decisions more and more by being in our inner world, listening to our true source, our lives begin to change. The outer life begins to change and reshape itself based on our direct connection to God. Sometimes relationships which are unhealthy, which lack joy and love, are simply dropped. Sometimes these relationships are with friends, spouses, or even mothers, fathers, brothers, or sisters. Sometimes God may say to us, about our mother or father or closest relative, "Let go, let God." Being born into a biological family which is devoid of love, joy, and health may be our lot at birth. It is not necessarily our lot for life.

Sometimes the still small voice will say *stay connected to our family and friends and learn how to love someone who is in deep denial of their true source and is very confused.* Sometimes the still small voice will say *drop them, leave them, let them go.* Thus, circumstances such as these will be different for every person, perhaps every time, for every person has their own lessons to learn around love. All we can do is to listen to God every moment and ask counsel and guidance. We will not find guidance outside of ourselves any longer. We are being asked to go to a higher place, to recognize the Divine source that exists within each of us.

Listening to the still small voice will take commitment, discipline, and practice. And the still small voice may not always be heard as an audible sound. It may be heard as knowingness, or intuition, or a feeling, or visions. God will communicate directly to each of us in the most appropriate manner and this could be differently at different phases of our lives.

And yet there are many other voices that speak to us, and all of these other voices may be called the separation. The path each person will take and the lessons they will learn are individual to them. How one person will learn to discriminate God's voice within them, versus another person, will be different. The techniques, teachers, process any one person will use and be completely successful with may be totally inappropriate for the next person. Only the still small voice within will know the right path for each of us.

What will be true for all of us is what we must offer God in return for hearing the sacred voice within us. First we must open our hearts in love to God and then we must give ourselves time to hear God. This means quiet time, alone time. Time when we go away from the hustle and bustle of the world and all of our worldly connections and relationships to go within and to hear God. This time will look different for each of us. For some it will mean meditation, alone, in front of an altar we have created in our homes. For others it will mean a daily walk in the woods, or it could mean a simple walk to the mailbox on a long country driveway. And for others it will mean a solitary fishing trip, or it may mean sitting in church praying. The form that we place ourselves in to hear God will not matter. We just have to use our inner sense of where it is easiest to hear God and to choose those forms that naturally allow us to feel our love of God and bring us peace and harmony.

Along with the time we give daily to hear God, we must also give our commitment and discipline. We must commit to a daily time and discipline ourselves to fulfill the commitment. The time, the commitment, and the discipline of daily listening to God will always be necessary. The form will change over time. The length of time may change over time. The ease of hearing God will grow over time. The commitment to hear God daily cannot change, for then we have turned from the sacred voice.

Over time, our meditations with God and our listening will begin to extend beyond the time we have set aside. Slowly we will begin to hear God at other times in the day, or at the most unexpected times. There may even come a time when our meditations with God are where we live entirely, and the time we spend outside of those meditations is only a small part of our days. There may even come a time when we realize we are *living in God* every moment of our lives, and we realize we are One with God. With this will also come the realization that the still small voice of God has led us home.

The following meditation will help you in experiencing the still small voice of God which speaks to you from deep within your being.

"1 Am the Still Small Voice Within You"

MEDITATION TO HEAR THE STILL SMALL VOICE OF GOD

INTENT

This meditation will assist you in hearing and experiencing the still small voice of God which speaks to you from a place deep inside of you, from your Godself. Through letting go of busyness, quieting ourselves, becoming still, detaching ourselves from our emotions, and opening our heart to God, we become aware of the still small voice of God within.

SUGGESTED ENVIRONMENT

Find an environment that is very warm and nurturing for yourself and which will bring you the greatest peace and comfort. This is very important, for it will give you the safety you will need to go within your being and to feel at a deep emotional level. It could be done inside in a quiet, darkened room, with a candle burning to symbolize the *Light of God*. If doing the meditation alone, ensure it is a place where you will not be interrupted or distracted. Keep a journal handy in which to immediately write down your experiences, visions and feelings so you can review them regularly.

HOW TO BEGIN

Begin with the following steps:

❧ First, find a comfortable position where your spine can be straight, either in a comfortable chair or lying on the floor.

❧ Second, close your eyes and do some simple deep breathing for a few minutes, releasing everything that has occurred previously in the day. The deep breathing is very important.

❧ Third, adopt an open, meditative attitude by simply reaffirming to yourself that you are open and listening to God.

❧ Fourth, focus your attention on the moment and quiet any lingering thoughts. Just become aware of your breathing and your body. Repeat the following affirmation (or one of your own) to yourself silently: "I Am Open To

Listening To God." If you are a visual person, try focusing on an image of a shining white light. When you feel complete begin the following meditation.

THE MEDITATION

With your eyes still closed just feel your body for a few minutes and again begin to breathe deeply, breathing out fear and breathing in love. Now place your attention at your head and slowly become aware of each part of your body, starting with your head and moving down to your face, neck, chest, arms, stomach, legs, and feet. Make a mental note of anything your body is telling you. Now feel your body as an instrument of Divine creation. Feel deep inside of yourself the sacred covenant that exists between your life and the Creator. Before you incarnated and God breathed life into your being, your soul and God reached an agreement and a sacred covenant was created for your sacred life.

Speak these words aloud or silently, three times:

"God, Please, Reveal Thyself To Me Within My Being. Please Speak To Me Of Our Sacred Covenant, Lord. I Am Ready To Hear Your Still Small Voice."

Do this meditation whenever you wish to connect to the still small voice of God and until such time as you are guided to do a different meditation. For some, this is a beginning meditation and they will only do it once.

Chapter Seven

The Dawn Of Tomorrow
"My Light Is Coming"

God has placed within each of us His divine love, His divine wisdom, His divine guidance. The *Light of God* which has now begun to descend upon our earth plane has come for all, not just for some. It is an individual choice as to whether we open our hearts to the coming *Light of God* or remain closed to it. It is through opening our hearts that we can individually prepare ourselves fully for what is to come.

Humankind in its present stage of development is like rough, raw gold ore. It must be sifted and refined before it becomes the pure gold of God consciousness. Out of the ground, out of the earth, humankind has sprung forth by God's call, God's evolution, God's process of breathing life into dust. It is God consciousness which creates and has created evolution, an aspect of the life force of life. Humankind is still evolving, evolving towards full God consciousness, and like this rough, raw ore, God continues to sift, refine and evolve man's present consciousness. God will continue to do so until only the pure gold of God consciousness remains.

The dawn of tomorrow will truly be a miraculous experience. It will be a tomorrow when every human soul will honor only the Master within, and within will become the miracle of without. From within each fully God realized human soul will flow heaven on earth. All will vibrate to God's tune and the illusion and separateness of self will have long since disappeared. Humankind has just entered the dawn of this tomorrow, the coming of God's light.

It is important for all souls who have chosen the path of God consciousness to keep their focus on this vision of the future and the coming of God's light. As the dawn of the present age turns to morning, then afternoon, and finally evening, the process may be hard and trying at times. Always the process will be glorious. The intense vibration of all souls on the planet becoming fully One with God consciousness will be beyond the human imagination or experience. As the dawn breaks on this present age of God choice and God consciousness, the pace of everything will quicken and vibrate faster.

For souls not choosing the path of full God consciousness, nothing really needs be said. Their choice will be honored by the Creator, and they shall forever through eternity be Loved. The Creator does not love by choice or condition, only by BEING.

God consciousness will speak to everyone from within themselves, and each will be given God's love and God's truth. As God consciousness evolves human souls, each will be asked to express God's truth and love through their thoughts, words, and deeds, through their life itself. Each will be asked to sing and dance their life force, their God consciousness, as the birds sing their joy daily.

The animal life on the planet are good models for the naturalness with which humans should be willing to express God with abandon, with love, with their all. And yet when one animal takes the life of another animal, humanity is to know the evolution of the animal has not proceeded as far as the human soul. And yet God evolves all, evolves all animal life, all human life. All are in different stages of life. All are together to learn and teach.

Today humankind is being asked to grow beyond itself. God asks us to focus on God fully as the way to know how to be in a relationship, how to form an institution or how to create a government. God asks us to trust God first and then act accordingly. If we were to recognize within ourselves the seeds of full Christ consciousness, of full God realization, we would hoard our individual personal life force and use it to focus fully on the Christ within, we would give the seeds of Christ within our full attention. In that act of self–empowerment, we would have chosen the path to our highest future, our highest moment.

The pace of humanity has quickened greatly in the last two hundred years. The quickening pace of humanity is reflected both outwardly and inwardly. Whenever there is an outward reflection, there is an inward generation. Wherever there is an inward generation, there is an outward reflection. That quickening first took place on an inward level and subsequently was manifested outwardly; outwardly in the industrial revolution, the invention of electricity and, eventually, computers.

There has always been, and will always be, an evolutionary energy within every human heart that is God created. Every human heart responds to these evolutionary messages. These messages that exist within the human heart are as if, at the appropriate time, God whispers in our ear where our next step will be. All of us, in a sense, hear these evolutionary prompts in different ways and respond accordingly in different ways. Our response is subject to our openness to God and to our own soul's spiritual development, where we are on the infinite spiritual spiral of God.

Humanity finds itself in a new age. An age where God's evolutionary prompt is being activated in all human consciousness. It is truly a miraculous sight to see this wave of God as it travels through humanity's consciousness, like a swell upon the ocean. At some point we realize what the present age is all about; it is simply God calling to all the children. God is asking us to hear God, to come home to God, to follow God. God is calling to all of us in a very personal and very empowering manner. God is calling to us from within ourselves, from within our consciousness as a still small voice.

It is as if a sacred voice has gone out on the planet from God and it can only be heard within. The voice is saying, *Behold A Sacred Voice Is Calling, All Over The Planet, A Sacred Voice Is Calling*, and it is God simply calling to all God's children on the planet.

From that place of true source that exists within every human being comes the true voice. Hearing God then becomes a simple matter of creating space in our lives, quieting ourselves, and simply listening for God's voice within ourselves. Everyone will do this differently, the technique or hearing of God within does not have to be the same, any more than people need to feel or look the same.

In addition to sending each of us a sacred voice to assist and guide us on our life journey to wholeness, God has also sent a holy light, an *inner holy light* that will lead each of us from our darkness. God asks that each of us follow our *inner light*, for that light will lead us home. When we contact our *inner light*, it is as if a great light shines forth before each of us.

In order for each of us to see the holy light that shines before us, we must take the time to see it. Just as with the sacred voice within, we must take the time to hear it. Our inner holy light is most easily experienced when we look deeply into another human being's eyes. When we do this the holy light shines forth from deep within our being illuminating the other's face, and we begin to see life as God sees it. We begin to feel life as God feels it.

When we take the time to gaze, slowly, openly, penetratingly at anything, we begin to perceive the holy light that God has caused to shine forth now in all our lives. In seeing this holy light in our lives, we do not always see with visual images, although we can. Sometimes we will see the light as a deep, shifted feeling within ourselves, as if we have transcended our bodies and are dwelling in another reality. And we are; we are dwelling closer to God. Sometimes we will see the holy light as deep joy, deep ecstasy, deep connection. Sometimes as flowing tears, as a giving away, or as a coming together. Sometimes as a deep feeling of belongingness to God and God's family.

As the sacred voice speaks from within our being, not always in words, so the holy light will not always be seen with our eyes. When we become aware the holy light is shining, we may know it, or feel it, or even hear it, and at times we will see it.

By focusing on God's still small voice and our inner holy light in deep meditation, we will be brought to completion. We have all the basic tools we need for our journey home to God. It is as if the sacred voice within is a road map through the wilderness, telling us where to turn, when to slow down, when to speed up, when to stop, so as not to fall off the cliff. It is as if the inner holy light is a flashlight that helps us see the darkness we walk in so we don't bump into a tree or another traveler, or walk off the cliff.

Humanity's spiritual evolution is poised for a great leap, a great spiral upward. It is simply time for humanity to take a great step forward in its spiritual development, in its ultimate unfolding of God consciousness. The ideas and feelings that are now traveling through the sea of humanity are not random occurrences. They are sparks that have been triggered in all human consciousness.

Not all have responded to these sparks, not all have chosen to. And within the personal experience of hearing a personal call from God, there is much room for confusion, fear, self-righteousness, and separation in the personal human reaction. However, what we see as the present age movement is the sum total of the evolutionary prompts that have traveled through individual human consciousness and hence the collective consciousness.

There is a new vision that is being shaped for humanity. It is a vision that is inspired by the Spirit that dwells within each soul. That vision places the personal relationship each of us have with God as the true source from which all manifestations of outer life flow. It does not create our outer life from our outer experience, for that is the cycle which humanity is just completing.

In the trust and vulnerability each of us will bring to our own personal relationship with God, we will experience a great joy, deep love, and, at times, a complete ecstasy. Within that experience our outer relationships will mirror this inner personal relationship. The communities of the future, the sum total of inner and outer personal relationships, will also mirror this inner experience of joy and love.

The future is pregnant with joy and love for humanity. Joy and love which will occur with the individual person on the most intimate and profound level. An experience which we will not read about, hear about, or be lectured about, but rather one that we will feel and experience in all parts of our being.

Collectively, humankind today has strayed far from its natural place of balance and centeredness. They have strayed far from the natural place of being in tune with the earth and hearing all its prompts and guidance. They have strayed far from the natural place of being in tune with one's body, ingesting the right amount and the right type of food. They have strayed far from the natural place of being in tune with one's emotions, knowing who one is and who one isn't. They have strayed far from the natural place of being in tune with one's mental environment in a balanced manner. They have strayed far from the natural place of hearing His voice and seeing Her light.

And yet this is the vision God has for humankind, to regain the inner balance, the inner naturalness. We must first walk individually in balance in a place of centeredness before we can walk there collectively. We must proceed to help the earth and humanity from a place of love and not from a place of fear and anxiety. To try to assist the earth or others from a place of fear only perpetuates the damage that has already been done.

Thus the process of unfolding this new vision for humankind is occurring now. This evolutionary process is evolving us from an extreme state of unbalance to a high state of balance. To prepare ourselves individually for this future we must do our individual work so we can release the inner blocks that keep us from opening our hearts to all, all the time. We must prepare ourselves mentally, emotionally, physically, and spiritually for God. We must open our hearts to the deep love that dwells within us and let it move from deep within our being outward, sweeping out all of our accumulated layers of fear.

The vision that God has for humankind starts with

the vision God has for each of our individual lives. The highest state we can attain in this particular incarnation is for our life to realize God's personal vision for each of us. The process of realizing that vision is the process of following God's personal guidance for our lives. For it is only by listening to God and following God that we will find God. And yet many people have found God with no awareness that they were even listening to God or following God. They were trusting themselves in following their life path, their heart, their own path of the heart, and when one trusts oneself deeply, one tunes in to this place of God that exists within our being.

The manifestation of this vision God has for tomorrow is simply the collective manifestation of the vision God has for our own personal lives. As God has described a life of deep love, joy, connection, and reverence for each of us, so has God described this same thing for humankind. Imagine being connected to everyone friend and stranger, animal and plant, the stars, the earth. Imagine feeling ecstatic joy when you awake in the morning and through every event that occurs in your life. Imagine feeling reverence and respect for all creation, knowing that God dwells within all form, vibrating it to creation and perfection. Imagine the outpouring of love that will occur when you feel this for everyone in your life and they for you.

Imagine taking a trip, moving through different spiritual communities on your journey to your destination, and always being welcomed by total strangers in a deep place of brotherhood and sisterhood. Imagine staying with these communities for as long as your Godself guides you. Imagine knowing that these new spiritual brothers and sisters will welcome you and trust you. Imagine every spiritual community that exists at that time, trusting their connection with God to the point where they welcome total strangers as brothers and sisters. Imagine every community that exists at this point, having as one of their spiritual practices the welcoming, the feeding, the lodging of total strangers. Imagine every community knowing that every traveler God sends, God sends as a teaching or a giving or as a healing. Imagine every traveler who finds himself at a community knowing that God has directed him there for a teaching or a giving or a healing.

These communities are in the future of humankind. They will exist and they will spring forth into manifestation. Their seeds are stored in the spiritual families that God is gathering together on the planet now. Now individuals are feeling the call to gather in spiritual families and to sit with like-minded and like-feeling brothers and sisters. Later, from these spiritual families, God will begin to create spiritual communities of like-minded and like-feeling brothers and sisters.

The purpose of these spiritual families first, and later the spiritual communities, will be to nurture our individual relationship with God. The families are a source of nurturance and softness for our individual God unfolding. A gentle atmosphere will pervade these families as well as a gentle harmony of interaction and activity. For the Christ consciousness will be directing each from within in their relationship and activity within the family.

The spiritual families as well as the eventual communities will be without ambition, for ambition is of the human consciousness. Their only purpose will be to nurture the hearing of God within and the unfolding of the Christ consciousness in every heart. These spiritual families will become a church by their very existence. They will not necessarily form a church and build a church building, they will be THE CHURCH by gathering as a family to hear God's voice and to unfold the Christ consciousness within. Each family will be the church and each family can be known as the church of the still small voice.

These spiritual families that are beginning to gather now are important, for stored in the hearts of members are seeds of light. God has stored seeds of light that will sprout as humankind's present consciousness, and civilizationswill move forward through cleansing and transformation. From these seeds of light that God has stored, a garden of light will grow through their coming together. Each family and eventually each community is a base camp for God's lightworkers who will sow more seeds of light. Like all gardens, it is important to allow it to receive water, compost, sunshine. Remember, God is doing the planting, not us. If we try to choose the people, we may be taught lessons. Only God knows which vegetables and flowers should grow together so as to nourish one another.

As these spiritual families gather and open to hearing God's voice within and to following their inner guidance, then all will realize that everyone sits equally before God. There will be no master, no leader, only God in each heart guiding.

Each spiritual family will honor all spiritual masters as an expression of God and all religions as paths to God. All the saints, all the masters, all the angels, all the people of love and the great Master Jesus Christ have been sent by God to lift us upward to light, love, and to peace. Each spiritual family will honor and respect other family members' relationships with the Creator.

Each family member will acknowledge that all can hear God's voice within them, and so members will not to look to another for guidance, they will look inside themselves. Each family will support and assist each member to facilitate the hearing of the sacred voice within themselves, calling upon all the techniques of all the religions and sacred energy of all the spiritual masters ever created by God. All spiritual practices, or ceremonies or rituals that have ever been given to humankind have been given, originally, directly by God *to all, not just some.* They may have been passed down through generations or specific cultures, but they come from God and must be shared with all. Humankind does not own what God has given, no matter who, how or where it was given first.

These spiritual families will place emphasis on love as the only place of real power and safety. In times of crises, pain, and upheaval in the physical or emotional plane, family members will be guided to turn to the God within themselves, not to the family or to other people. In the gentleness and safety, family members will heal all their wounded parts. Emphasis will first and foremost be placed on love. Even clarity is secondary to love. For from love, healing flows, and from healing, clarity. Clarity is a by–product of healing and healing is a by–product of love.

The dawn of tomorrow has come and heralds the coming *Light of God*, the coming of the greater Christ Light, a Light that will illuminate all darkness in us personally and on the entire planet. The Christ Light is like a powerful medicine that God is giving to us to heal all of us and to expand all of us. The following meditation will help you open to the coming Light.

"My Light Is Coming"

MEDITATION ON THE COMING OF THE LIGHT OF GOD

INTENT

This meditation will assist you to open yourself to the coming of God's Light so you can have your own personal sense of it and know how you can prepare yourself for it.

SUGGESTED ENVIRONMENT

This meditation should be performed at dawn or in the early morning. Dawn is a powerful time both in an energy sense and also symbolically. It can be performed out of doors or indoors. One could sit facing east, perhaps with a candle in front of you, in a comfortable position. Perhaps you may want to stand up and face the rising sun if you are outdoors, with your arms outstretched as in the illustration on page 101 of this chapter. If doing the meditation alone, ensure it is a place where you will not be interrupted or distracted. Keep a journal handy in which to write down your experiences, visions and feelings so you can review them regularly.

HOW TO BEGIN

Begin with the following steps:

🌿 First, find a comfortable position where your spine can be straight, either in a comfortable chair or outside sitting on the ground.

🌿 Second, close your eyes and do some simple deep breathing for a few minutes, releasing everything that has occurred previously in the day. The deep breathing is very important.

🌿 Third, adopt an open, meditative attitude by simply reaffirming to yourself that you are open and listening to God.

🌿 Fourth, focus your attention on the moment and quiet any lingering thoughts. Just become aware of your breathing and your body. Begin to repeat the following affirmation (or one of your own) to yourself silently: "I Am

Open To Knowing Of God's Light." If you are a visual person, try focusing on an image of a shining white light. When you feel complete with this part begin the following meditation.

THE MEDITATION

Close your eyes and see a vision or a mental image of the bright shining sun coming up over the horizon. Just focus on this image of the rising sun for awhile. Now become aware this bright shining sun coming up is within you and focus on it arising in you.

This coming of the Light you are watching within yourself is the true dawn, for it is the holy *Light of God* and it has begun to shine forth before you. Allow yourself to feel this sunshine within you as love, joy, comfort, safety.

Now open your heart fully to the sun and speak these words aloud or silently three times:

"Creator, Shine Your Holy Light Before Me. And Reveal Your Vision Of My Life To Me. How May I Serve You, For I Am Ready For Your Vision."

Do this meditation infrequently and only when guided.

Chapter Eight

The Christ Within

"My Work Is Not of This World"

God sent Jesus Christ to the earth plane to be the wayshower. Christ consciousness is God consciousness. Christ and God are the same, are One. If we could see deep inside of ourselves we might see a picture screen where we would view Him, talking to us personally. This would not make our personality, our outer self, God or Christ. It just means He is blessing each of us, nourishing us, helping us, and loving us through our human experience. And deep within us He exists and a mystical and transcendental state of a full union with Him awaits all. If we are to fully serve Him we must be able to open to His Presence within ourselves.

Jesus was given full God realization in His life by following the Christ within. In following the Christ within every moment, He opened to and became fully God realized. Jesus, in becoming God realized, in becoming Christ conscious, showed the way for all human beings. Jesus Christ was the seed which God planted on the earth. When Christ was born, God planted the seed of Christ consciousness and Christ light within every soul. For the last two thousand years this seed has been germinating in the human consciousness, nurtured and tended by each individual gardener. Thus, within each human soul, this Christ consciousness was planted, for within, so without; for without, so within.

At this dawning of God consciousness, it is time for this seed of Christ consciousness to begin to sprout forth. In the sprouting forth, the tree will eventually bear the fruitage of the Christ mind, the Christ behavior, the Christ words, the Christ thoughts, the Christ feelings, the Christ consciousness.

It is, indeed, a glorious future that God has in store for his children, a future of miraculous and blessed events. A great dance is being planned for earth's children, a dance where all will be invited and most will come. A dance where all will dance to the same tune and rhythm, those who do not dance will learn, they won't be able to help it. They will hear the music within their being, they will feel the rhythm in their bodies, they will see their partners dancing and deep within themselves they will begin dancing to God. They will dance to a state of rapture, of ecstasy, of boundless and endless joy. They will dance to God and in this great dance, the dancers will become One with God. In this happening the Christ consciousness of many souls will burst forth; in their moment of full God realization they will create an event unlike any other. It will have the brilliance of a million, million stars and it will be felt throughout the Universe, throughout God. All the Universe will experience it as a shudder, and will know what has occurred.

Two thousand years ago when the Christ consciousness was brought by Jesus, the forces of fear were very strong, and yet weak enough for the Christ consciousness to be given birth. Now the forces of fear are even weaker overall and yet more concentrated in individual human souls. It is within our fertile ground that the seed of Christ consciousness was planted.

We are all gardeners of this Christ consciousness within ourselves. God has planted this seed within each of us and given us the responsibility to nurture it, water it, love it, and do what is necessary in our being so when it is time for it to sprout, it will sprout within each of us.

No one else is responsible for this individual sprouting and flowering of Christ consciousness within our being. We cannot give this responsibility to our mates, our priests, our friends, our teachers, our gurus. It is our own personal responsibility. Nor can we take another's advice or teaching on how to bring to sprouting and fruition this Christ consciousness within; we must listen to the teachings of our God source within and knowing thqt God speaks from within all.

In God's love for every human soul which has chosen to be separate, God has given the power to create a self, a personality. God has also given each soul the power to know how to come home to Oneness, to realization. Within each heart, each soul, the knowledge of how to make the journey to Christ consciousness exists. In truth there is only one message and that is God, and yet everyone's path on the earth plane is different. There is only one destination for all five billion souls on the planet and yet there are five billion individual ways to get there.

Each gardener must turn within to hear the precise gardening instructions that will allow Christ consciousness to burst forth within them. What is appropriate in one garden is not necessarily appropriate in another's garden. There is only God's sacred voice from within our heart that will guide each of us to Christ consciousness. God speaks to each of us in many languages in many ways within our consciousness. It is through the gentle guidance of the sacred voice within our hearts that we will be led to wholeness.

Love is the unmanifested expression of the Spirit divine that resides at the core of consciousness of every human being. It is the brilliant white light that many humans experience when they have opened themselves to who they truly are and who is creating their human concept of who they are in any moment.

Love is the manifested power of Spirit. It is the true power of the Universe and it is the intelligence that flows within every particle of form ever manifested. It is the Creator's vibrancy that knows of no illusion, that knows of no fear, for there is only whole and complete power. There is only perfection and the experience of perfection. Within the experience of perfection the Creator's divine love is expressed. When a human being experiences this divine love, enlightenment, samadhi, ultimate realization is created.

The human consciousness may open to love in many different degrees, and any individual human consciousness is in a process of evolution towards divine love. Every individual human consciousness has been given a will to decide for itself the manner, the degree, the time it will open fully to divine love.

Nothing stands between a human consciousness and opening fully in any life to Divine love other than choice. Habitually, human consciousness chooses worldly aspects to prioritize and to give great importance to rather than God, thus delaying their full opening to the Divine. By continually focusing on the material plane, you choose not to focus on love. You choose to be right rather than loving, you choose to be comfortable rather than loving, or you choose to be materially abundant rather than abundant with love. And so you are, in any moment, at your highest present state of evolution, and there is always more. There is always full opening to the Divine love that exists within each individual at any moment.

Christ consciousness dwells within each human being. That consciousness is waiting patiently within every human heart for its time to burst forth. Waiting as a mother patiently waits for her child to grow into a mature adult, ever nurturing, ever giving, ever loving. Christ consciousness exists within all humanity, for God planted this seed within *human consciousness*. The birth, death, and resurrection of Jesus Christ has a deeper meaning for each of us rather than a simple birth. It is a reflection of what is to come within all human souls.

The sending of Christ to the earth plane and His life and the bringing of true love and light was one of God's greatest gifts to humankind. In that gift, God planted Christ within every human soul that ever was, is, and ever will be. Two thousand years ago the explosion of light and love was outside of all humans on the planet, save One, Jesus Christ. All others watched this Divine expression.

It is now time for the seed of Christ within to burst forth on the earth plane of every human soul who chooses to open. Christ consciousness is real, Christ consciousness is within, and it is now time to allow oneself to open fully to His divine glory. Knowing that Christ is within, waiting to burst forth, does not make you Christ. But He is within you, guiding you and helping you. Will you obey, will you listen to Him? It is through the *inner Christ* that we can do

His work in the world. Remember, His work is not of this world.

Sometimes the human consciousness has become confused on where Christ consciousness exists. Jesus knew Christ consciousness existed within. He would go into the desert continually and commune with Him directly. Through His life, Jesus came to a total state of oneness of the Creator within. In opening fully to what was within himself, He showed the way for all people. Within every human heart, Christ dwells. Opening our hearts opens our consciousness to the Christ within and is the key to unleashing Divine love.

Divine love is the truth, and human feelings are the doorway to the truth. Opening to the human emotions that call to us in any moment is the doorway to the love within us. The emotions both point the way and form the doorway which we must pass through in order to access the bottomless well of love that dwells within each human heart.

The emotions we experience are like a thin film of oil on the surface of the deepest part of the ocean. We must go through the film to break the surface of the water within ourselves to access our deepest part. If, however, we are put off by what the surface looks like and wish to avoid going into the water, then we lock ourselves out from the deepest part of ourselves. Alternately if we feel that our emotions are caused from without, by another person, we lose all conception of ourselves. At the point human consciousness feels something and blames something or someone outside themselves for causing it, a disconnection occurs. This disconnection from the true source within is experienced as extreme pain and hurt.

Once the disconnection occurs, the human consciousness exists in a state of blame and judgment which only causes the disconnection to become more pronounced. Within this experience much human suffering is perpetrated. Indeed, the disconnection from the true source within and the actions which ensue have been characterized throughout human history as evil. Disconnection in any human heart is never done with intent; always, it is done out of ignorance, confusion, and patterns of habit. In the darkest, most confused person exists the miracle of the Oneness, waiting patiently for the human consciousness to turn within to the inner light.

When human consciousness lives in a place of Oneness with the Christ within for any length of time, physical, mental and emotional changes take place. Likewise the vibratory nature of the human form changes, and this new vibration attracts new vibrations. Thus, often times our friends, relationships, acquaintances change as we open our hearts in deeper ways to the love within ourselves.

The Christ consciousness is very close to the earth plane now. The Christ consciousness would like those who worship in God's name to begin frequently gathering together in circles, in homes, in places of work, in nature, wherever. These are to be informal circles of people with no leader and no priest. Rather, all are to sit equally before the Christ within.

These gatherings are to occur with the intent of connecting to Christ, to feel Christ, to see Christ, to hear Christ, to experience Christ. There will be many miracles that will occur and many miraculous experiences that will happen at these gatherings.

It will be helpful if, when people gather, they leave behind their past spiritual experiences and their intellectual sureness of what is and what is not God. The Christ consciousness would like people to gather in God's name now, in humbleness and in love of God. The Christ consciousness would like them to bring their childlike innocence and wonder and awe to these gatherings.

The Christ consciousness would like to begin speaking directly into the hearts of people who gather in God's name now. The Christ consciousness has a personal message for all and specific guidance for everyone on the coming changes. Each of us has our own work to do and our decisions to make, so the message that God wishes to bring is for us and us alone. The Christ consciousness wishes to speak directly to our hearts so we can hear Him from within our being, so that there will be no mistaking His words.

One does not have to be a member of any religious organization in order to hear the Christ consciousness. One simply must open their heart in love to the Christ consciousness. All who love Christ will hear Christ speak to them from within, there are no exceptions. People may gather to simply hear Christ, they may gather to ask for a healing from Christ, or they may gather and ask for a teaching from Christ. Whatever, it is important to simply gather in Christ's name now.

These circles are to be simple gatherings, they are informal, there is to be no ambition to these gatherings. People are simply to bring their love and innocence. These circles can be anywhere at any time for any reason. These gatherings have as their only purpose to bring like-minded and like-feeling people together in God's name.

The times that we are in are times of transformation, times of cleansing, times of healing. It is important for each of us to learn how to connect to Christ's energy and Christ's consciousness. It will be a source of continual support and guidance in our lives for the times ahead.

The Christ consciousness invites all people of all religions to gather in God's name now, and the Christ consciousness sends blessings to them, whatever their path. People who gather in this manner need not change their religious path, need not join a religious organization. They need not do anything different with their lives, only to hear Christ's words and gentle guidance within themselves. The

Christ consciousness asks people to gather in God's name now, not for reasons of religion, rather for reasons of wholeness and love.

The Christ consciousness also invites people who gather in this manner to bring to these gatherings their religion, their saints. It matters not whether a group of Hindu peoples gather or a group of Buddhists. The Christ consciousness invites the Hindu peoples to continue to pray to Krishna at these gatherings and to also feel the Christ that dwells within them. The Christ consciousness invites the Buddhists to continue to meditate on Buddha and also to meditate on the Christ that dwells within them at these gatherings. The Christ consciousness invites all people of all paths to gather now in God's name and to continue the spiritual path they are on. The Christ consciousness simply asks people to open to the Christ that dwells within them now.

Remember, Christ will judge all religions alike as to whether they have kept His word and loved God above all and loved their neighbor as themselves. The belief system that God favors only some, rather than all, will not survive the coming of the *Light of God*. This belief system must expand to see God's love in all, everywhere and at all times.

We cannot, in our human limitations, understand that the Christ Spirit is never divorced or separate from bringing love into the world. To be imbued with the Christ Spirit is to love all of our brothers and sisters in the world as we love ourselves, as we love Christ Himself. It is a practice for us, it is our spiritual practice to love those who condemn us or criticize us. If we love Christ and we wish to kiss His hand, for He is our Master, then we are guided to be kind to people. When we are kind to a person then we are kissing the hand of Christ directly. That is how we demonstrate our love for Christ, by demonstrating our love for each of our brothers and sisters. As Christ comes into our lives, our humanness must be let go, for Christ's teaching and vision for humanity is not of this world.

Our work now is to open to God's love and the Divine wisdom that dwells within each of us. As we open to that which exists within us, we will give it more and more space in our lives to blossom forth. God is very present within us at this time on the earth plane.

All the spiritual truths that have been written throughout human history by all the masters by whatever path they took have come directly from God. God has spoken these spiritual truths from within their being. The fragrance of these spiritual truths has varied but never the essence. God has spoken in many different languages to many different masters, and always His message has been the same: to love all, to love God, to feel God within yourself, to see God within all creation, and especially to love your fellow human beings.

Our work on earth is to love. Our work here is to love all that God brings us each moment. God is the truth. There are no other truths. We are all here on the planet to help each other open to God by feeling love for each other and allowing connection to take place with one another. When we stop our openness with one another, we stop the expression of love. When we stop the expression of love, we stop God and then we don't do what we are here to do, which is to love.

Only two things are needed in life. One is to choose to feel love every moment, the second is to open to God and follow God's guidance. These two actions go hand and hand. They are the two most powerful actions a person can initiate. Love is the fuel, the catalyst for opening and realizing God consciousness.

Love and truth also go hand and hand. Love and truth are the building blocks of a healthy group or a healthy relationship. Without love one cannot nurture oneself, one cannot heal, one cannot provide safety or feel safe. On the other hand, without truth, one cannot expand, one cannot see beyond the moment to the inspiration. To have one without the other is to be blind or deaf, to have both is to have all of one's faculties.

Focusing on the Christ light that dwells deep within our being will bring the light to the surface so that it will pour out of us. Creating space for the Christ light in our life will empower it so that the small candle flame deep within us grows to blazing proportions and pours out of us.

The Christ light that is in each of us is not owned by anyone. One does not have to be a member of any organization in order to open to Christ's light within. One can experience Christ in a deep meditation or even in a long walk in nature, as well as by reading the words Christ spoke. The Christ light within each of us is a personal gift from God. This inner light is a reflection of our sacred relationship with God that exists within each of us.

So many human beings have been wounded by religious organizations, all in the name of God. God does not wound, God only loves. Man wounds and uses God as his excuse for wounding. To wound someone in the name of God is to dwell within the human consciousness, not in God consciousness. A closed heart, like a closed fist, offers no space for love, offers no space for light. The constriction of a closed heart is like a piece of steel; nothing can pass through it unless it is broken. And so, those whose lives are painful and full of suffering must examine their heart for its openness. At times, cleansing and letting go are necessary, for only then can opening take place, for healing to occur and love to dwell. Love must have space, must have openness to dwell in our lives.

Unless a closed heart chooses to open and release the clenched fist that exists within it, it will be broken. For only in the breaking can the opening of the heart occur to allow greater love and light to dwell within the consciousness. The tighter the constriction of the heart and the more determined the human consciousness is not to open the constriction, the greater the breaking that must occur for the love to dwell within.

God wishes to break no hearts, only to love. It is the individual choice that creates the breaking by the degree and depth of constriction. The opening of a heart can be done very easily, very softly. Children do it all the time. Dogs and cats are constantly opening their hearts no matter what the circumstances. Forgiveness is a key to opening a closed heart, forgiveness of our selves, of others, of our perceptions of injustices, real and imagined.

The Christ consciousness is like a breeze blowing across the planet and its fragrance is being detected by many people now. Soon this Christ breeze will become a great wind and all will feel it. It is time to gather in circles and honor the Christ consciousness that dwells within each of our hearts and the hearts of all people. In these gatherings and in these circles it is important to be respectful of each person's individual relationship with God. The Christ consciousness asks us to begin gathering in Christ's name now and to experience Christ within ourselves.

The holy light of Christ that we each have is buried deep within our heart and it is in our heart that we can commune directly with Christ. By focusing on our inner light we empower our relationship with the holy Christ and so our inner light becomes brighter and stronger, for it is He who is empowering us. By communing directly with the light of Christ within and obeying His command to offer only love, we strengthen our inner relationship with Christ and grow in our own Christhood, thanks not to ourselves, but thanks to His loving grace and His light. It is He who enlightens us when we dwell on His light within and begin to empty ourselves out in the deep silence of our being.

The following meditation will assist you to connect deeply within yourself to the Christ Light which burns brightly.

"My Work Is Not of This World"

MEDITATION ON THE INNER <u>CHRIST LIGHT</u>

INTENT

This meditation will assist you in connecting to the Light of Christ which burns brightly within your being and which is ever present within you to guide you, heal you, and love you. The inner Christ light has only one intent and that is to love you beyond your wildest dreams. When Christ was born, God planted the seed of Christ light within your soul.

SUGGESTED ENVIRONMENT

Allow yourself to be guided to a nurturing and quiet place to do this meditation. Find an appropriate position and sit quietly, taking a moment to feel your body, your breath and the moment. If doing the meditation alone, ensure it is in a place where you will not be distracted or interrupted. Keep a journal handy in which to write your experiences down so you can review them from time to time.

HOW TO BEGIN

Begin with the following steps:

✺ First, find a comfortable position where your spine can be straight.

✺ Second, close your eyes and do some simple deep breathing for a few minutes, releasing everything that has occurred previously in the day. The deep breathing is very helpful.

✺ Third, adopt an open, meditative attitude by simply reaffirming to yourself that you are open and listening to God.

✺ Fourth, focus your attention on the moment and quiet any lingering thoughts. Just become aware of your breathing and your body. You could repeat the following affirmation (or one of your own) to yourself silently: "I Am Open To The Inner Christ Light." Keep a journal handy in which to write down your experiences, visions, and feelings.

THE MEDITATION

With your eyes closed, allow yourself to see before you Jesus Christ, standing with His arms outstretched, bathed in a glorious white light and bathing you personally in His white light. Honor your own perception of what the Christ light looks like, for your vision comes directly to you from Him. Or you could see or feel a brilliant shining white Light or Star of Light; or the Sun as if it was next to the Earth itself. Now speak these words aloud or silently three times:

"Oh Christ, Light The Fire Within My Soul. I Am Ready To Open To Your Light Within My Being, And I Commit To You Now And Evermore."

Do this meditation whenever you feel guided, and also whenever you feel battered by life, or confused, or whenever you do not feel the light of the Christ within you.

Chapter Nine

The Christ Without

"You Have Much Work To Do For Me"

*O*nce we have connected to the light of Christ which is deep within all of us, we are then able to offer it out to our brothers and sisters, mates, friends, pets, the entire world at large. It is only through a direct inner connection and communion with the Christ, within our being, that we have anything to offer to anyone. For when we dwell constantly and continuously in deep communion with Him, it is He who expresses through us and we allow our human self, our personality, to drop away so only He shines forth. All of us have much work to do for the Christ light; coming together in the light, rejoicing in the light, working together in the light.

Christ wants us to love each other and to love ourselves. For it is through love that He can communicate to us through other people. It is through love that His messages can be received and given, for His message is only love. Love opens the channels between people so that God– so that love–can flow easily between them. Our job is to love one another here. Christ asks us to follow the path of love and joy as we go about being obedient to His inner guidance. He will guide us and show us the way and each of us alone must choose how we walk. Only by walking in love and joy can we let our old selves die, no matter what is asked of us and no matter what challenges are brought to us.

Remember, Christ is within all and Christ speaks through all. Focus on the inner Christ within a person and you will hear Christ speaking directly to you. Do not make distinctions between what is and what is not Christ in another. See only the Light of God, see only the Christ, listen only for the Christ and you will only experience the Christ, and in your experience you will serve Him in a personal and individual way. Remember, relationships are the vehicles to connect to the Christ without. It is through your relationships that you either turn your back on Christ or you welcome Him into your heart and to your home. Do not avoid your relationships and do not turn from them. Welcome all into your life as if Christ has sent them directly to you, for He has.

When we begin to perceive the light within another human being we have begun to perceive the light within ourselves, for another's light is merely a reflection of our own light. Remember, the Christ light is within all and all are assisting you to realize your own light. It is a trap to only want to seek light in another and ignore the seeking of light in ourselves, especially when it is done out of fear or guilt. The seeking of light in another or within ourselves must be done out of joy, out of love, out of surrender to God's goodness. The light cannot reach us from the outside through the steel doors of our personality. The light can only shine forth from deep within our being, and only by shining our own light, can we let another's light in.

The clearest way to focus on another human being's light is to focus on our own light. If we never fully feel or see our own light, it is not possible to see another's. If we choose to make another's light more important than our own light, we have lost our connection to our own light.

If another person is kind to us, we must use the experience to focus on our inner light so we can only see light in them. If they are mean to us, we must use the experience to focus on our inner light so we can only see light in them. We must use all of our worldly experiences, all of our outer experiences for focusing on our inner light. Only then do we serve the light, all light, whether it is our light or another's light, and there is only one light. Thus by going deep inside our inner light, no matter what our outer experience, we give power and true meaning to the words, "There is only the light within me."

We must also understand that the Light of Christ and our inner light are the same holy light. And yet it is as if Christ is the sun come to earth and we are the light of fireflies floating near the earth. We have something of His Light within us and yet the scale is beyond human comprehension. By preparing ourselves, by walking His way, we open ourselves to the possibility that His Light will enter our little light and we will expand beyond all recognition. This is what has happened to all the saints and enlightened masters that have dwelt on our earth plane. God's Light has entered their light and expanded it beyond all human boundaries.

Another distinction to understand is the difference between the light that is here now on the earth plane and the *Light of God* which is coming. It is as if you are flying a kite and the kite needs wind to propel it, to raise it off the ground and the wind is the light. Today, if you focus on the light within, it is as if you are taking your kite for a Sunday fly. When it is all said and done you will have a nice day and your kite will rise very high. The coming *Light of God* is like a Divine Hurricane, the greatest Wind ever spawned, so much wind that it is again beyond comprehension. This Divine Wind will take your kite and raise it farther than you can imagine. And yet if you happen not to be flying your kite that day, because your heart is closed or you have turned from the light, you will miss this Divine Wind. It is time for you to focus on this coming *Light of God* by opening your heart to all God brings to you through all those around you and so that you will be prepared for what is coming.

As goes the inner experience of each human conscious-ness so goes the outer experience, and it is always our heart which does the talking for us, for our tongue is connected to our heart as our eyes are connected to our soul. For the inner experience and the outer experience are One. It is only in the state of separation that one can even distin-guish between an inner and an outer experience. To God consciousness these distinctions do not exist. It is the life within that creates the life without. If one's life without is filled with angry people, hateful people, painful people, then they are merely reflections of the inner pain.

Generally the human consciousness does not know how to look within its being and see the levels of separa-tion it holds. In its separation, the human consciousness almost always focuses without on the outer form of an-other. Human consciousness is mesmerized by the display of separation which exists in separate human and physical form.

Human consciousness draws to itself both the light

and the dark that it is either incapable of looking at within itself, by itself, or which it judges within itself. When the human consciousness can gaze at its own light and dark, it frees itself and expands. The fear of looking at oneself often times is too great to gaze upon. Further, the fear of having the fear can thwart the releasing of the fear, although never stop it once a soul is committed. It is fear of fear that locks us out of our very own spiritual progress. Many times when a killing or a taking of another's life occurs, it is because it is too painful for one human being to gaze upon a reflection of itself, so it destroys it in the hope it can be kept away.

Further, when outside events occur and we choose to suffer out of ignorance, or another attacks or criticizes us and we choose to feel fear, these are choices of the personality, of the outer self. The inner self, the higher self, our Godself knows only light. We may always choose, from the inside of our being, the light. Sometimes it is helpful to continue to repeat to ourself the words, "There is only the light within me, there is only the light within me," softly, over and over to ourselves, throughout the day, and especially through trying circumstances.

When we are being attacked our fear will come up. If we can continue to focus and repeat these words, "There is only the light within me," we will make our light more important than our fear, we will make our light more important than the outer experience of attack, for we will have made our inner experience of light paramount.

There is little accountability in gazing at another human form and seeing qualities that one judges as bad or distasteful. In our small seed of Christ consciousness, all of us are true clear mirrors and each allows everyone else to reflect ourselves back to us. Whenever we focus on an aspect of another human being that needs to be helped or fixed or changed, and we can't draw our attention away, it is a flag for our own growth. It is a sign that this aspect is a place in us we are either not aware of, or else a place we do not choose to work. Thus we feel that if we just change that aspect in another person it will be changed in ourself, and, of course, that is never the case. Even if we remove that person from our life, another will come into our life with the same aspect to reveal ourself to ourself.

Whenever we focus on an aspect of another human being's outer self, it is the gyrations of the personality. The personality is not capable of going very deep into one's own being. That is why spiritual practice is often called a discipline or a work, for it takes focus, personal energy plus time to penetrate through the outer, surface layers of our being to our core. The outer layer of the personality is not actually very deep and not very strong, even in the most hardened case. And yet it is like steel doors on the outside, almost impenetrable, but on the inside it is like a soft cloud, easily gone through. This is because the light shines from the inside out for all of us, and so where the light shines, the form is soft and pliant. We have no choice on the light shining from within, for God shines light from within every one of us.

From without there may or may not be light shining on us, depending on how well or how poorly we have surrounded ourselves with nurturing relationships, or friends, or places to live, etc., and depending on the life lessons we have come here to learn. From within our being there is always light shining, for that is the light of the Creator creating creation—you. No matter how awful or tragic our outer life is, there always exists a bright shining light within us, deep within our being.

No matter how awful or impenetrable the steel doors of our personality are from the outside, we can go through them softly, quietly, easily from the inside of our being. We must simply find the light that exists within ourselves and allow it to lead us out through all of our layers through the strait jacket of our personality.

The process of finding God's light within ourselves is one of looking inside. It is taking the time to look inside for the light and to look consistently and constantly. After a while subtle changes begin to occur. The light becomes brighter within us and we become softer inside. Over time the steel doors of our personality soften, perhaps to wood, then to curtains. Eventually, if we focus on our inner light long enough, the clouds on the inside become clouds on the outside and soon they part and the most amazing bright shining sun comes out.

Thus, this process of focusing on the light that dwells within us cannot be overemphasized. It is how we will realize God on the earth plane. By focusing on our inner truth, on our inner light, we will eventually bring the light outside of us, so that it will shine forth from our being. This light is not our light, this light is God's light, we have just become the empty vessel, the instrument here.

When the doors of the personality have passed from our lives, then our light will shine forth to all eternity. For when this occurs there is no filter holding back the light within. Whenever the light shines that strongly from within one human being outward, all other human beings who feel that light, feel the light of God upon themselves. Our work here is to find this light within our being, this light that God has placed in every one of us. Once we have found it we are to let it shine out of our center.

When we have let the light within ourselves become that strong, we have made our light more important than our personality, we have made it more important than other people's personalities. Our light has become the most important thing in the world, more important than mates, parents, friends, objects, houses, or pets. When we have let our light become that strong within us, we are in the world but not of it. The world ceases to hold our attention. Another's personality holds no interest. We may observe it, but it is not worth commenting on, for we are fully focused on our light.

When we make our inner experience of the light more important than anything else that is happening in the moment, we open ourselves up to miracles. Whatever the outer experience, the inner experience of light will transform it. We will not transform it, the light within us will transform it. For in that moment we will have chosen to make the Creator more important than anything else in our lives, and when we have done that, we transcend our human experiences and dwell in a very, very high place.

Eventually, by continually choosing to make our inner light more important than any of our outer experiences, we become fully, every moment, our inner light. We become God realized, we become our Godself, for we have chosen not to block the expression any longer of our inner light. It is not a matter of learning how to seek our inner light, it is a matter of choosing our inner light and spending time experiencing it.

It is time now to focus on the light within each of us, and the clearest way to see another's light is to focus first on our own inner light, our own Godself. By feeling our light, we slowly let it out from inside. As it comes out, so will the truth of the words we speak, the loving nature of our actions, the gentleness of our thoughts.

In allowing the light to come forth from our being, we allow it to resonate outward, like an energy wave. As this energy wave travels outward it resonates within another human being, activating their own inner light. Even through the steel doors of their personality the light travels. The light can travel where words or actions or thoughts cannot.

In feeling our light we will behave according to the light, speaking and acting from our place of light. We will be giving our highest self to another, for we will be in touch with our Christ consciousness. In allowing our light to come forward we will then be able to see another's light clearly and cleanly. No matter what the reaction of another to feeling our light, we can deal with it from a place of light, for we are fully focused on our place of light and can feel our light.

The light that we focus on within ourselves is God, is the Christ consciousness, is God's love. By focusing on our inner light we allow ourselves to become an instrument of the light within. By focusing on God within, on the Christ consciousness, we allow God to shine forth through us, we allow ourselves to become an instrument of the Christ consciousness.

All people on the planet are holy, for they all have the seed of Christ, of God, within them. They are all sacred brothers and sisters. The birds are holy, all the animals are holy, all that swim in the sea are holy, all that fly in the air, all that walk on the earth. All have an inner light; all have the seed of God within them.

When we focus on our seed of God within, we will resonate with the seed of God that exists within all other forms. When we commune with our own light we will commune with everyone else's light. When we talk to our own light we will talk to everyone else's light. When we listen to our own light within we will hear other people's light.

The following meditation will help you to connect to your inner Christ light so that you may see and experience only the light in another.

"You Have Much Work To Do For Me"

MEDITATION ON
THE CHRIST WITHOUT

INTENT

This meditation will assist you in first connecting to your Christ light and second in letting it flow outward from the center of your being. This meditation will assist you in being in the world but not of it.

SUGGESTED ENVIRONMENT

Practice this meditation anywhere at any time, more often the better. If you were to practice it every moment of your life, a great miracle would happen. Keep a journal handy in which to write down your experiences, visions and feelings.

HOW TO BEGIN

Begin with the following steps:

🖖 First, find a comfortable sitting position where your spine can be straight.

🖖 Second, close your eyes and do some simple deep breathing for a few minutes, releasing everything that has occurred previously in the day. The deep breathing is very helpful.

🖖 Third, adopt an open, meditative attitude by simply reaffirming to yourself that you are open and listening to God.

🖖 Fourth, focus your attention on the moment and quiet any lingering thoughts. Just become aware of your breathing and your body. Try focusing on an image of a shining white light.

THE MEDITATION

With your eyes closed repeat the following words, either aloud or silently to yourself for ten minutes:

"I Am Dedicated To The Light Within Myself,"

or the words,

"There Is Only The Light Within Me."

Now sit quietly for a few minutes and open to any experience of visions which the light brings you. Bring up an image or a feeling or think about someone or a situation in your life that you are having a hard time with and simply focus on them as you feel the Light, allowing yourself to see their Light. Try to do this daily in deep meditation, or any other time you think of it throughout the day, especially out in the world as you go about your daily business.

Chapter Ten

And God Created All People Equal

"Service To Me Is Service To All"

*O*ur Divine Parents are creating all and the Divine is within all. When we focus on the creation, then we see only the shadow on the wall, while when we focus on the Creator within, we see the truth, the essence of the creation.

No one is separate from God and yet the illusion that all are separate is a very powerful force in the world today. God has created all people equal in God and none are outside of God, yet there is the appearance that some are and some are not. This is the power of the illusion of separateness. By focusing constantly and purposefully on seeing the Creator within all, we can cut through this illusion like a hot knife through butter.

In all creation all is equal, for all is God consciousness. Within every human soul, every blade of grass, every rock, every tree, every animal, every known and unknown physical form in the Universe, rests God consciousness. In that spark of God consciousness everything is equal, there is just the Oneness and love of the Creator. How can one piece of God consciousness be more or less than another piece of God consciousness, especially when it is not possible to even separate God consciousness? Separate consciousness is human consciousness.

All form has evolved from God consciousness. All form is but an illusion created by the separation from full God consciousness. And yet the illusion is real because the human consciousness has given form power. There will come a time on this planet when the human soul will cease to give form power and will instead give power to the only true power, God's love within.

The flowering of individual form to God realization and Christ consciousness is a blooming of our True Self. Who can say a rose is better than a gladiola and say anything? Both are individual flowerings of the God consciousness brought to full realization by the Creator.

Do not look on the physical form of another human being, focusing on the surface differences, and expect to see anything of value or meaning. Individual form is an illusion that washes forth and away as waves on an ocean. God has created every loving soul in God's image of light and love, full and whole. If you were to gaze upon your soul with your earthly eyes you would be amazed at its brilliance and the intensity of how it shines forth.

The Creator has also created every living soul equal. As you gaze upon the soul of another human being, all there is is light. Deep within yourself is God, and deep within the heart of every other human being on the planet is God. God is the true source of every human being on the planet. From this true source comes all the manifestations of form, form which manifests as physicality, emotionalism, personality, even psychicality. All are aspects of form which come from the one true source.

When each soul incarnates, it is seeking the light; it is seeking to merge fully with the Creator. The experience of human life is a doorway all souls must pass through in their upward evolution of full God consciousness. In the upward evolution the human soul must burn off or purify all of its past karma or past debts. Or rather, must confront all of its illusions and realize its true nature. This process of a soul confronting its delusions and realizing its true nature, its Oneness with the Creator, this is called life.

A life of a soul is the life of a human being. All souls seek to return home to the Oneness. The personality and all other aspects of physical form are simply the vehicle the soul has chosen in Divine relationship with God to realize Oneness.

All souls work in Divine relationship with all other souls. All souls mirror their perfections and imperfections and illusions through physical form to each other. When a soul can gaze upon human hatred and see beyond it to the light and love of God within and see the true source, then that soul has let go of the imperfection of hatred within itself. Having let go of the illusion, the soul will not attract it any further into its human consciousness.

When the human consciousness, which is a manifestation of the soul, can gaze out on other souls and see only God, that soul will see what God sees. All creation has come from God. We must respect creation, for God has created it all. We must respect each other, for God has created each of us.

So often in human history the human mind has gazed out on all it saw with a closed heart and, from that place of closed steel doors, has judged, has expressed, this is right, this is wrong; has judged one aspect of life better than another aspect; has judged one person or a whole country of people less than another, or less than themselves.

To judge another, or any aspect of life, as good or bad, is to disconnect ourselves from our heart, from our place of God within. To disconnect from God around any issue is to call in increasingly harsh lessons, for our souls desire ever to expand upward, seeking more and more to open to the light. These lessons come in order to open our heart to that aspect within the world, and ultimately within ourselves, which we have judged.

When a person steps away from his personal accountability, opening to all his or her darkness, then the darkness will be manifested outside of the person and the lessons become harsher. When a country steps away from its personal accountability and closes to the darkness that exists in the collective consciousness, then the darkness will be manifested outside, usually as a war.

When a woman ignores the healing of her relationship with the Divine Father, she will manifest this unhealed relationship outside of herself. Likewise when a man ignores the healing of his relationship with the Divine Mother, he will manifest this unhealed relationship outside of himself. When a person ignores the healing of his or her fear of their animal nature, then the fear will be manifested outside of the person. The fear may seek to kill or torture animals or nature in general, whatever.

These unhealed parts within a person may manifest as unhealed relationships in many different forms. Control, domination, constriction, fear, negativity, are all symptoms of these unhealed parts within ourselves. They are there to call our attention to our own healing; they have nothing to do with another person other than the bringing of keys to our own healing. Again, when a person attracts another person who is intent on changing something in the first person, it is because that first person wants to change that piece in himself or herself but doesn't know how, or is avoiding his or her personal healing work. When two people are involved, the lesson is for both, never just for one.

When we think something, we send out an attraction to link to another thought; that's how thoughts get linked together to form coherence. God chooses which thoughts to link, and thus, in a sense, creates our reality. Thus, if we think of a tree, we might then think of something from childhood or from yesterday. God chooses whether it is a childhood thought or a thought from yesterday and so chooses which thoughts to link. Likewise, God chooses which people to bring into our lives and whichevents to occur all for our healing and God realization.

One of the greatest gifts we can give our fellow human beings now, at this point in the transition of consciousness, is respect for who they are and their personal life process. Who they are on the outside, in their personality, in their lifestyle is a reflection of the relationship they have inside with their light, their source. Whatever that relationship is, constricted or expansive, we must respect it, for it is their relationship. Each of us, every one of us, has a direct, personal, intimate relationship with the Creator, who dwells within us. That relationship is sacred and we are all sovereign in that relationship. It is important to respect each other.

In respecting every person and their life journey we will learn how to respect all creation, for all is holy. The earth mother is beginning to cleanse herself now. This is a natural process which God within Her form is directing. The earth is in good shape, as the earth was here before humankind and will be here after humankind. What is important now is that humankind learn how to tread on the earth from a place of centeredness, from a place of balance, from a place of light.

Many people wish to help the earth now as they pick their heads up for the first time and gaze around at all the destruction and devastation that exists. The destruction that the earth has suffered at the hands of humankind is too obvious to ignore anymore. Even in its obviousness, it continues. There has been little shift away from the continued gorging by man and woman. And yet it doesn't matter, for the earth will heal; it will heal through its storms, its earthquakes, and through all of its earth changes.

Will humankind heal? That is the question as the transition of consciousness occurs. Even today, with those who seek to assist the earth mother in her cleansing, much harm and destruction is done in the name of wholeness. When humankind seeks to correct environmental abuse from a place of fear, only more destruction occurs.

It is being out of balance which has caused the destruction in the first place. Let all who seek to help the earth, first learn how to walk in balance in their lives. Let them seek and find their own light and once they have done so, their words and actions will flow from this light.

Much destruction occurs today in the name of good as does much destruction in the name of God. When man or woman acts from his or her personality, they act from their surface, from their most shallow place. When man or woman act from their Godself, their light, they act from the truth, and the actions and the words will have a decidedly different feel and look to them.

All that is of the earth is of the Lord, all is holy, all is sacred. All is equal before God, there are no exceptions. A right action taken from a place of woundedness and fear becomes tainted by the fear and loses its rightness. On the outside no one may see, no one may know; on the inside God knows, God always knows.

Let those who would save the earth first bring peace to their lives. Let them first find their inner light and dwell in it, their inner joy and sing it, their inner peace and be it. From this place within, the quality of the actions outward will flow. We are all loved equally by God, all creation is loved equally. It is time to open ourselves to the Creator within all creation.

It will be helpful at this time to begin to address the Creator when we interact with any form. If we are cutting down a tree, ask the Creator of the tree for blessings. If we are planting a garden, ask the Creator within the soil for blessings and also the Creator within the seeds we are planting.

If we are preparing food, ask the Creator within the food for blessings. If we are nailing a board, ask the Creator within the hammer and the wood for blessings. If we are interacting with another person, ask the Creator who dwells within their heart, perhaps silently to ourselves, how we can serve the Creator in our interaction with this person.

In short, begin a constant dialogue with the Creator so that we may open our consciousness to God that dwells within everything. In opening our hearts, our minds to God within all, we will open ourselves fully to the God consciousness which is waiting patiently to come forth in a blaze of light in each of our lives.

The following meditation is a starting place for you to begin your intimate conversation with our Creator.

"Service To Me Is Service To All"

MEDITATION ON CONVERSING WITH GOD

INTENT

This meditation will assist you to begin conversing with God in all. By dialoguing with the Light of God in all, you will know how to serve God with all. From deep within all people, all animals, all trees, all rocks, and all known and unknown physical forms in the Universe, the Light of God emanates forth. In the Light of God all is equal and by seeing only the Light in all, you will serve the Light in all.

SUGGESTED ENVIRONMENT

This meditation should be practiced first in a quiet and nurturing environment which you have chosen. Once you have established a dialogue within yourself with God then it may be practiced anywhere at any time. When first practicing it, ensure it is a place where you will not be interrupted or distracted, and write your experiences down in a journal.

HOW TO BEGIN

Begin with the following steps:

    ✹ First, find a comfortable position where your spine can be straight, either in a comfortable chair or lying on the floor.

    ✹ Second, close your eyes and do some simple deep breathing for a few minutes, releasing everything that has occurred previously in the day. The deep breathing is very important.

    ✹ Third, adopt an open, meditative attitude by simply reaffirming to yourself that you are open and listening to God.

    ✹ Fourth, focus your attention on the moment and quiet any lingering thoughts. Just become aware of your breathing and your body. Begin to repeat the following affirmation (or one of your own) to yourself silently: "I Am Open To Having A Conversation With God." If you are a visual person, try focusing on an image of a shining white light. When you feel complete with this part begin the following meditation.

THE MEDITATION

With your eyes closed, gently allow yourself to float up out of your body to the ceiling of the room you are in, or above your body if you are outside. Now look down on your body sitting or lying there and focus your attention on some physical aspect of your life whether it is a person, an object, the earth, a tree, whatever, and allow yourself to see the Light of the Creator emanating from it. Now with your focus on the Light emanating from within it, say aloud or silently to the Light three times:

"Creator, I Send My Love. How May I Serve You?"

Simply be open to your experience.

Once you have practiced this meditation alone and feel you have opened a dialogue with God's Light emanating from all form, then begin to practice it any moment of the day you think of it. So if you are nailing a board, simply talk to the Creator within the board, then within the hammer, then within the nails. Again, simply say to the Creator within each of these:

"Creator, I Send My Love. How May I Serve You?"

After a while you will begin to hear answers within yourself from the Creator of the form, from God.

Simply begin to address the Creator within all form, whatever the circumstances, whatever the form. Do it as often as feels right. These dialogues should be done silently within. Also, when you feel you want to share what you are hearing, or check your motive, see if the Creator within you is guiding you to share or not to share or whether you are prompted by your ego self, your personality.

Chapter Eleven

The Future Is Now
"Follow Your Own Light, It Will
Lead You Home To Me"

*N*ow is the preparation time for the coming of the *Light of God* and receiving the word of God directly within your being. There is no more time to avoid our personal relationship with the Creator. Now is the time to put purposeful attention and action towards developing an inner relationship with your Creator.

Spend time alone communing directly with the holy light which God has placed directly within your being, spend time jointly communing with God, and above all obey God's personal Guidance to you which will come from attuning yourself to the still small voice within. Now is the time to purify yourself and you can only do that by obeying God in thought, word and deed. Trust the Divine that is creating you this very moment. God asks that each of us follow our own light, for that light will lead us home to Him.

It is time to acknowledge our individual journey toward God, whatever its form, and to start our spiritual work. Humanity is entering a transition of consciousness and this will be manifested outwardly from our collective inner experience. When humanity experiences a critical mass of people who are following God in their daily lives, moment to moment, then a significant shift in the collective consciousness on the planet will occur. The future is now, it is simply time for each of us to make our choice. It is time for each of us to do our individual emotional and mental clearing and physical and spiritual purification following our inner guidance.

Now is the time for each of us to be fully accountable for all of our thoughts, words, and deeds. Now is the time to look within to seek the inner Christ Light, the savior, the God consciousness. The time has passed of looking without for another human being to bring us to fruition. Now is the time for each of us to take a close look at our individual lives, lives filled with love and pain, hurt and joy, anger and gentleness; to look deeply at all of our individual life experiences and to discern the greater spiritual meanings.

No one can do the future for us. Only we can, individually, with our individual lives. No one can pull us from our sleep, our illusions, only the "I" that speaks to us from deep inside our being can. No matter how long the process of full accountability takes for our lives, it is one of the steps that must be taken along the journey to Christ consciousness. We must choose the path of God consciousness. We must open ourselves to our inner being and work with all parts within ourselves, both the light and the dark.

We must be fully aware as we take this journey that it

is the spark of God consciousness that makes life possible. We must also not be lured into believing that other people have the power to speak for God consciousness about our personal life in place of that still small voice within our very own hearts, and we must remember God speaks *to all*. Everyone who opens their heart in love can hear the sacred voice within. It is time to allow ourselves to hear that sacred loving voice. Only within ourselves, deeply buried within, is our connection to the One.

It is time for all human beings to open to their deepest parts of love and light within themselves. It is time for all who are on the planet to choose to become, or not to become, direct channels for divine love. The rapture is close by; the decision each human heart must make to choose God cannot be put off any longer. If the human consciousness decides not to decide, the decision has been made.

There are many souls on the planet now. There are more souls on the planet now than at any other time. There will be a vast display of love and light on the planet very soon. Souls have come, hungry to connect in this most powerful way with the Oneness in physical form.

All souls seek the Oneness and full God consciousness in human form. Each soul in its wisdom creates for itself the physical form and human experiences which are designed to lead it back home. And in the designing of the life experiences whose intent is to experience divine love, the human consciousness exists as the vehicle. The human consciousness at times resists this journey toward full God consciousness and at other times embraces the journey. At times human consciousness expands ever upward to spiritual bliss and harmony, and at other times it contracts down to pain and suffering.

It is time to begin to create space in our lives, in whatever is the appropriate form, to foster the sacred relationship that exists within us with God. By choosing to feel and hear the Creator within us, we will begin to experience God. God will guide each of us into the next century and into the next step of our evolving consciousness. God will guide us to a new role in life, to new relationships and new friendships, to new places to live, to new ways to earn our livelihood, to a new life. The key through all of this is to let the outer form of our lives be created from within, from our inner sacred relationship with God. In this way we will be fed by our experience.

God may well direct us to take up a specific career or to take up a particular spiritual path. However, if we decide for ourselves that we wish a specific career and are successful, our experience will not feed us. Our success, our actions will not bring fulfillment, it will bring more inner hunger and hollowness. So we must still our minds and open our hearts to the Spirit which dwells within us.

Deep within our being is a personal message for us from God. This message will unfold to each of us our life's work, the purpose of our incarnation. Each of us have come here at God's pleasure. The Creator has given life to each of us. We are here only to serve God. God is the Master, the true Teacher, we are God's children.

We cannot hear this personal message from God unless we go within ourselves and allow space for it to unfold. The highest life we can choose in this incarnation is the life God has already chosen for us. The clearest progress we can make in this life is by following the path that God has already chosen for us.

The Creator within our being has already chosen for each of us the spiritual practice that is most suited for us. God has already chosen for each of us the spiritual direction that is most suited for us. God has already chosen the spiritual mate that is suited for us. God has already chosen the spiritual family that will nurture our inner God relationship to the greatest extent. God has already chosen what our highest career is at any given time. God has chosen for us our highest life. By connecting deep within our being, we can open to God's choice. We will never clearly hear God speak of these choices outside of ourselves, for that would be to invite abuse from the human consciousness.

Most importantly, deep within our being, God has placed loving guidance on the great gifts God has lent us for this incarnation. Whether they be gifts of healing or teaching or prophesy or entirely new gifts, the information of these gifts is stored deep within our being. It is as if the Creator has dictated a personal message to each of our souls and placed it there until such time as we are ready to hear it. Unless we seek this message and these gifts within ourselves, we will never find them, we will never realize them.

We must be willing to open ourselves to the Creator within. Usually we spend our lives opening to everything but the Creator. We open our lives to other people, we open our lives to teachers, to books, to television, to our careers, to all manner of worldly events and circumstances. Somehow we must find it within ourselves to set all these worldly events aside and open ourselves to ourselves, to our true self, to God that dwells within. Once this is done God's guidance will be heard within our being. God's message will be felt within and we will know God's plan for our lives. God's gifts will become obvious and we will begin to heal, or to teach, or to do what God has given to us.

Now is the time to open, the future has become the present and unless we make our choice clearly within ourselves now, the opportunity could be lost for an entire lifetime. It is important to evaluate our lives, to take stock of them and to be clear about what does and what does not nurture our relationship with God. Those circumstances, relationships, or whatever, which take us within ourselves and support our relationship with the Creator should be noted. Likewise those circumstances and relationships which take us outside ourselves and do not support our relationship with the Creator should also be noted.

Those aspects of our physical bodies which support the clarity and health and purity of our human temple should be noted, as well as aspects which do not; likewise, our emotional patterns and mental processes. Also, we should note our work atmosphere and whether or not it supports our inner relationship with God.

There will be many changes that will come with the transition of consciousness that humankind is entering. All material form, all human consciousness will experience change in this great transition. The degree of our individual change, the quality of it, and the ease of it will depend entirely upon our inner relationship with God. If our inner relationship with the Creator is flowing and fruitful, honest and also full of integrity, we will fly with the transition of consciousness. We will thrive and we will experience these times as glorious.

Again, God has sent each of us very powerful gifts for working with this great transformative period. God has sent the sacred voice which will speak deep within our being to us, guiding us higher and higher through the worldly storms. God has sent the holy light that shines forth before each of us. A holy light that will lead each of us from our darkness into light. These are very powerful tools and the power of the Creator is connected to their use. In placing these tools deep within our being and encouraging each of us to open to them, God has given us no reason to receive our inner guidance through another person. Rather, God's guidance for our personal life can bubble up as a clean, clear cold mountain spring within us, where it is not subject to another's interpretation.

The future is now. It is time for us to look within and begin to express with our lives that which we are hearing and seeing. It is time to come into full awareness of the gifts the Creator has given each of us and how the Divine wishes us to use them in this life. It is time to hear God's personal message.

The following meditation will help you to hear a personal message from God and you will hear it spoken from deep within your being.

"Follow Your Own Light. It Will Lead You Home To Me."

MEDITATION TO HEAR A PERSONAL MESSAGE FROM GOD

INTENT

This meditation will assist you to connect to a personal message from God which has already been placed within your being, concerning your individual spiritual journey through life. God asks that each of us follow our own light, for that light will lead us home to God.

SUGGESTED ENVIRONMENT

Create an environment that is very warm and nurturing for yourself and which will bring you the greatest peace and comfort. This is very important for it will give you the safety you will need to go deep within your being. It could be done inside in a quiet darkened room, with a candle burning to symbolize the Light of God. It is best to do this meditation alone, so ensure it is a place where you will not be interrupted or distracted. Keep a journal handy in which to write down your messages.

HOW TO BEGIN

Begin with the following steps:

❧ First, find a comfortable position where your spine can be straight, either in a comfortable chair or lying on the floor.

❧ Second, close your eyes and do some simple deep breathing for a few minutes, releasing everything that has occurred previously in the day. The deep breathing is very important.

❧ Third, adopt an open, meditative attitude by simply reaffirming to yourself that you are open and listening to God.

❧ Fourth, focus your attention on the moment and quiet any lingering thoughts. Just become aware of your breathing and your body. Begin to repeat the following affirmation (or one of your own) to yourself silently: "I Am

Open To Hearing God's Message." If you are a visual person, try focusing on an image of a shining white light. When you feel complete with this part begin the following meditation.

THE MEDITATION

This meditation can be done as often as you wish. It is best done after a deep period of quiet time in meditation, and it can be done anywhere at any time. Just realize that in order to hear the message you must first go through many layers of your outer life in order to hear it clearly and accurately and your heart must be open in love to all.

Sit quietly with your eyes closed and meditate on the still small voice of God within you. To facilitate your hearing the still small voice, try listening deep within your being to your inner sound. First visualize or feel yourself going deep into a well that goes deep within your being to a golden river of light that flows through your life. On reaching the river, simply open yourself to the experience and ask the Creator to reveal to you your inner sound. Your inner sound is unique to you, it may be anything. The sound of Aum, or angels singing, music, the sound of a drum beat. Once you have connected to this deep level within yourself, speak these words aloud or silently three times:

"Oh Lord, You Who Have Been With Me Always For All Eternity, Reveal Yourself To Me. I Am Ready To Hear Your Message."

Write your experience down and share it with your spiritual family.

Chapter Twelve

❧

God Is Calling To All People In His Ministry

"We Have A Covenant"

G od has a calling for you personally. God has sacred work He wishes you to accomplish in your lifetime. It is your ministry, it is your purpose for being alive on the planet now. Open to God's holy light and God's still small voice and hear what He has to say to you directly. The sacred work He would have you do will bring you immense joy and pleasure, for through it you will align your being even more with His will. It is through serving God that you will be led home to God, there is no other way and it is the only way that will bring your heart and soul the intense love, joy and freedom it hungers for.

All human souls are God's ministers on earth. All people, through opening their heart and listening and following the still small voice and their own holy light, have a ministry to teach, or to heal or to express in some manner. The God consciousness that vibrates through our body, keeping our heart beating and lungs breathing does not ask permission to express. Nor does a human soul need permission to express God's love or truth.

Since everyone can hear God's sacred voice within them, and everyone has a ministry, then the net effect is simply God expressing God to God. Through this process the barriers of the human consciousness will fall and all will open to God consciousness.

So look within your heart, and listen very carefully to the still small voice of God. How would the sacred voice and the holy light have you conduct the ministry of your individual life? Perhaps no differently than you are doing, perhaps radically different. Perhaps you are to leave your mate, perhaps you are to reaffirm your life commitment to your mate, perhaps you are to look for a mate, perhaps you are to stop looking for a mate. Only God's personal guidance to you can lead you into a life lived fully with God.

The purpose of coming into God's *ministry of your life* is to express God. By calling forth all souls on the planet into God's ministry at this time, God brings forth humankind's next great expansion of consciousness. In the past humankind has looked upon a church building as a church, and a minister as a minister, and a congregation as a congregation. These are but reflections of the truth. God's church is all that is without–the earth, the houses, the people, the animals, the plants, the human body, the emotions. All that is without, all that is form, is the church. All that is within is the minister, and there is only one minister, and that is God himself. God speaks to His church, continuously, God can be heard as the still small voice within.

All life is God's church, all the Universe is God's church, the earth is God's church. All people are in God's congregation, all animals, all plants, all rocks, all are in the congregation. God speaks to all the congregation continuously, lovingly, with wisdom. All we need to do is to be still and listen within, God will speak directly to us.

One does not need to study with other human beings and be taught by other human beings in order to hear God's voice, although God may direct us to other people for this purpose or other purposes. God uses earthly teachers to help show us a different perspective in order for us to have a different awareness of ourselves, others, of all, and of God. God is the true teacher and respecting the earthly teachers shows respect for the teaching as well as for God who sent the earthly teacher to you. Only God is to be worshiped, for only God is the true teacher. Earthly teachers are instruments of God. They, like you, are all part of God's creation. Only God is God.

When you study with an earthly teacher, think of yourself climbing up a vertical cliff, struggling to climb to the top, feeling very scared, vulnerable and in a precarious state. As far as you are concerned there is only one way up this dangerous cliff-face and it is not easy or pleasant. At some point you become aware that there is someone standing next to you and in a flash of insight you realize you are not climbing up a vertical wall, you are merely crawling on the ground. The earthly teachers God will send to you will simply say, "Stand Up," and you will just stand up and walk away naturally from a new and higher perspective. God uses earthly teachers to help show you a different reality and only God is the True teacher. For any teaching, thank God first and above all, and remember God is within you.

Go deep within your being and open to God's voice. Go deep within and open to your inner vision, your holy light. That inner vision that the Creator has placed within you is your highest fulfillment in this lifetime. Your deepest level of empowerment is within your individual and unique inner vision. It is who you are at your highest level now. Tuning into your inner vision is to tune into the *ministry* that God has created and has waiting for you.

By allowing your inner vision to manifest and to express in the material world, you allow God to take you to your next highest spiritual level. You allow God to evolve you. Fulfilling God's vision for your life is how to become God's minister and to develop your ministry here on earth. The highest vision for your life comes from your highest aspect, the aspect that is deep within you in which God whispers to you in a still small voice. You cannot know your highest vision by listening to another, or to your parents, or to your friends, but only by listening deep within yourself to the Creator's voice.

In the future, the work of minister and ministry will take on a deeper meaning. At their deepest level, every human being on the planet is a minister. Each minister has a ministry and that is what each individual life is about. As ministers we cannot look outside ourselves for understanding what our life is about. For what our life is about outside is simply a reflection of how deep we have gone into our true source inside at that moment. The deeper we go inside into our Christ consciousness, the more the outer life will be transformed by Him through our inner work.

As our ministry unfolds, we must remember we have only a small part to play. If God asks us to be a bit player on a stage and bring a bucket of water onto the stage, then that is all that we should do. It is inappropriate to walk on and start singing, or add something to the play or use the water in some way we are not being directed. That may be up to the show's star or heroine to do that. Remember we are sent places to do one thing only and to do that the best we can and not to be the Messiah or the Savior, for that role has already been given to Jesus Christ. Nor to play God and try to create God's vision for our lives. We simply must be open to God's vision. Trying to create God's vision for ourselves will bring us untold misery.

Remember, God is directing your life process. Put your faith in God. If you can't obey the commands of the Divine Director. He will send you off the stage until you learn your lines properly, otherwise you will disrupt His play.

As I write this book I am filled with my experience of the still small voice of God. Indeed, the words of the book come pouring out from that part of my consciousness. Often times when I listen to the still small voice, I am swept away with emotion and tears begin to run down my face. I have simply connected to that place of overwhelming joy within.

Many times after I have connected to that inner well of joy within myself, I will honor the God within all I meet for hours after, in a sense, tuning into the God within all people and feeling my light and seeing their light. By focusing first on experiencing my own inner light, I experience a flow in my dealings and relations with other people. The inner light guides both of us in our relationship for God loves all. Although we experience the inner light separately, it is the same inner light.

As I meditate on how the still small voice wishes me to finish this book I hear, "Tell them of your own spiritual journey." As I go deep within myself and feel who I am, I can tell you I am a child of God. It was only through the Grace of God that I was lifted up out of my own confusion in my life and it was through following my heart, doing what I love that I connected to the Grace.

I can tell you I have always loved nature and have

always felt a great love of something quite beyond myself being in nature. I always followed my heart when it came to spending time in nature and taking time off from work. Nothing was more important to me than my love of the deserts, mountains, and seashores and my vacations there. It was through that love that I eventually found God. At first it was simple experiences such as being in a boat on the ocean and lazily watching eagles fly overhead and being filled with a sense of overwhelming joy and goodness. I felt God at those times and yet I did not know it was God I was feeling, I just knew I was feeling something bigger than me.

Eventually, by simply following my heart and what I love to do, I began working with a very gentle teacher of the earth. I was introduced to the drum and began to spend long periods of time in the wilderness alone. It was during those times that I became fully aware that God was speaking to me from within as a still small voice. The more I listened inside, the more my awareness of God grew, the more I began to feel, hear, and experience God in everything. At some point, Christ came to me in a vision while I was meditating and I cried, for I had never had such a personal experience with Christ. In my meditation, I had a vision where I saw someone sitting by the road. I knew it was Christ but this being did not look like the pictures of Christ or the way, perhaps, we want Him to look. In the vision I said, "Who are you?" The Being said, "I am Christ." I said, "You don't look like Christ, and yet I know you are."

And Christ said to me, " Sit down here, I want to talk to you about appearances and how deceptive they can be and how you must look past them to see Me in everyone." I was given a direct teaching about seeing the Christ in all.

In some of my other meditations I felt the presence of other Saints and angels from many different cultures and religions. I realized that God has sent many teachers to humankind, all with the intent of lifting us upward to light, love, and peace. I saw God's presence in all religions and I realized that all religions are gifts from God meant only to lift us up to His joy and love and freedom.

Later I began to spend much more time in the desert for it was a place of great natural beauty and I felt drawn there. It is so quiet and peaceful in the desert, I experience it as an outward manifestation of God's peace. I continued to listen inside myself for God's voice and the more I focused on this in my meditations, the stronger the presence of God became in my life. I began to listen to God's sacred voice and to follow His plan for my life, which led me to change my career of twenty years and to begin to tell others of the still small voice within and to write this book for Him. My personal experience is not a model for other people, it is simply one demonstration of one relationship with God and how I personally unfolded into His plan for my life. God's will directs each of us from the inside to our proper path to realize God if we will take the time to here meditate on Him.

There are many words that are written in this book and there is only one message. The still small voice of God speaks within every human being on the planet and within all creation. A holy light shines before each one of us. It is time for all of us to open, hear, and follow our Divine Guidance for our lives. It is time to feel the Creator within ourselves and to acknowledge the Creator within all. God has sent a holy light to each of us. That light will lead each of us from our darkness. God has sent a still small voice and a holy light. The *Light of God* is coming to our earth plane and now is preparation time for all. Through opening our hearts to all we will be prepared for what is to come.

The following meditation will assist you to discover what God's ministry is for you. We are all God's ministers, all five billion souls on the planet today and all people, through listening tos the sacred voice within, God's voice, can know God's personal path for them.

"We Have A Covenant"

MEDITATION TO REVEAL GOD'S MINISTRY TO YOU

INTENT

All human souls are God's ministers on earth. All people, through the listening and the following of the still small voice of God within and through the seeking of their own holy light, will allow themselves to become God's instruments on earth, allowing God to express through them. This meditation will assist you to open to the ministry God has already given you.

SUGGESTED ENVIRONMENT

Create an environment that is very warm and nurturing for yourself and which will bring you the greatest peace and comfort. This is very important for it will give you the safety you will need to go within your being and to feel at a deep emotional level. It could be done inside in a quiet darkened room, with a candle burning to symbolize the Light of God.

HOW TO BEGIN

Begin with the following steps:

   🌿 First, find a comfortable position where your spine can be straight, either in a comfortable chair or lying on the floor.

   🌿 Second, close your eyes and do some simple deep breathing for a few minutes, releasing everything that has occurred previously in the day. The deep breathing is very important.

   🌿 Third, adopt an open, meditative attitude by simply reaffirming to yourself that you are open and listening to God.

   🌿 Fourth, focus your attention on the moment and quiet any lingering thoughts. Just become aware of your breathing and your body. Begin to repeat the following affirmation (or one of your own) to yourself silently: "I Am Open To Knowing God's Will For Me." If you are a visual person, try focusing on an image of a shining white light or an image of Christ Himself. When you feel complete with this part begin the following meditation.

THE MEDITATION

Do this meditation only after you have done all the other meditations in this book. If you are doing the meditation alone, with your eyes closed, see yourself sitting with a circle of people you love and who love you. Focus on this feeling or vision. Now gently float out of your body. As you float up to the center of the room, look down on your body sitting or lying there. Now begin to hear God's voice within and see God's light within yourself. Now speak these words aloud or silently three times:

"Oh Christ Light Who Dwells Deep Inside Of Me, Who Always Has And Who Always Will, Show Me The Gifts You Have Given To Me In This Life And How I Can Use Your Gifts To Serve You."

Or, if you are doing the meditation with your spiritual family, sit in the middle of the circle of your spiritual brothers and sisters. They would sit around you with a candle in front of them, feeling love for you. You would be surrounded by light and the deep love of your spiritual family. Sit in the circle and feel God within you, listen for God's still small voice, see God's holy light, and speak the same words aloud.

When the ceremony is complete, have a dinner with your spiritual family. Share your experience, have them share theirs, feel love and joy, feel the mystery of the Lord. Do this meditation rarely and only when guided. Once your ministry and gifts have been revealed to you, God will refine them from time to time in similar meditations, God will direct you, directly. Trust your sacred connection with the Creator.

The End

A Review

The coming of the *Light of Christ* is signaling a new way for all of humanity to communicate directly with God. In this simple way, God's sacred voice can be heard as the still small voice within.

So can each of us, by focusing on communing directly with the Creator of the Universe, hear Him as the still small voice within, guiding us gently on a path of love and light home to Him. It is time for us, all of us, to realize that we can talk directly to God every moment and that God speaks directly to every person. Mostly, this dialogue goes on in our unconscious mind, for to be conscious of the dialogue, the following is necessary:

- **LETTING GO OF BUSYNESS**

- **INNER QUIETNESS**

- **STILLNESS**

- **STOPPING THE CHATTER OF THE HUMAN PERSONALITY, MIND, EGO**

- **DETACHMENT FROM ONE'S EMOTIONS**

- **OPENNESS TOWARDS GOD – CHOOSING GOD**

About The Author

Gary Spanovich is a lover of God who has spent a great deal of time in the natural areas of the Earth and devotes his life in service to God. Presently he writes and offers seminars on the meditations contained in this book. He also teaches at a small college and lives and gardens in the woods of the Pacific Northwest with his wife.

For those who are interested in the message of this book a Newsletter is published which you may subscribe to which chronicles the author's reflections and the results of his meditations on the still small voice within. Also, seminars are offered regularly, as well as longer term retreats.

If you would like further information on these activities and publications offered by Gary, please write him at:

Path Of The Heart 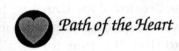 *Path of the Heart*
PO BOX 1067
Canby, Oregon 97013

Please include a *self-addressed stamped envelope* with the form below:

- -

NAME _____

ADDRESS _____

CITY _____ STATE _____ ZIP ____